D1547145

THE NEGRO IN
LITERATURE AND ART

AMS PRESS
NEW YORK

PHILLIS WHEATLEY

THE NEGRO

IN

LITERATURE AND ART

in the United States

by
BENJAMIN BRAWLEY

New York
DUFFIELD & COMPANY
1930

Reprinted from the edition of 1930, New York
First AMS EDITION published 1971
Manufactured in the United States of America

International Standard Book Number: 0-404-00139-4

Library of Congress Number: 75-144586

AMS PRESS INC.
NEW YORK, N.Y. 10003

To the Memory of My Father

EDWARD MACKNIGHT BRAWLEY

CONTENTS

Illustrations

Preface

"THE Negro in Literature and Art" is intended either for general reading or as a text for classes or clubs interested in the subject. The present edition offers some distinct differences from those of 1918 and 1921. In general it brings out the Literature, as compared with the Art, in bolder relief. As before, however, there is the effort to give comprehensive treatment to the more important figures.

The first chapter, and the sections on Mrs. Fuller and Mr. Braithwaite, originally appeared in *The Southern Workman;* and that on the Stage was in part a contribution to *The Springfield Republican.* The first of the supplementary sections gives in its entirety an article that originally appeared in *The Dial* of Chicago (May 11, 1916). The second is a portion of "The Negro in American Literature" in *The Bookman* (October,

1922), and the third is from "The Negro in Contemporary Literature" in *The English Journal* (March, 1929). All are here used with the kind consent of the owners of these periodicals; and it is hoped that the supplementary sections, taken together, will be found to give a review of the more important literature produced within recent years *about* but not *by* the Negro. Thanks are also due to Mr. Braithwaite and Mr. Johnson for permission to use some of their poems covered by copyright; to Dodd, Mead & Co., the publishers of the works of Dunbar; to Harper and Brothers for permission to quote eight lines from "Ballad of the Brown Girl," by Countee Cullen; and to Harold Vinal, Ltd., for permission to quote "I Closed My Shutters Fast Last Night," from "An Autumn Love Cycle," by Georgia Douglas Johnson. The bibliography has been given radical revision.

BENJAMIN BRAWLEY.

Raleigh, N. C.,
  July 1, 1929.

THE NEGRO IN
LITERATURE AND ART

THE NEGRO IN
LITERATURE AND ART

I

THE NEGRO GENIUS

IN his lecture on "The Poetic Principle," in leading down to his definition of poetry, Edgar Allan Poe has called attention to the three faculties, intellect, feeling, and will, and shown that poetry, that the whole realm of aesthetics in fact, is concerned primarily and solely with the second of these. *Does it satisfy a sense of beauty?* This is his sole test of a poem or of any work of art, the aim being neither to appeal to the intellect by satisfying the reason or inculcating truth, nor to appeal to the will by satisfying the moral sense or inculcating duty.

The standard has often been criticised as

narrow; yet it embodies a large and fundamental element of truth. If in connection with it we study the Negro we shall find that two things are observable. One is that any distinction so far won by a member of the race in America has been almost always in some one of the arts; and the other is that any influence so far exerted by the Negro on American civilization has been primarily in the field of aesthetics. To prove the point we may refer to a long line of beautiful singers, to the fervid oratory of Douglass, to the sensuous poetry of Dunbar, to the picturesque style of DuBois, to the mysticism of the paintings of Tanner, and to the elemental sculpture of Meta Warrick Fuller. Even Booker Washington, most practical of Americans, proves the point, the distinguishing qualities of his speeches being anecdote and brilliant concrete illustration.

Everyone must have observed a striking characteristic of the homes of Negroes of the peasant class in the South. The instinct for beauty insists upon an outlet, and if one can find no better picture he will paste a circus poster or a flaring advertisement on the walls. Very few homes have not at least a geranium on the windowsill or a rosebush in the garden. If also we look at the matter conversely we shall find that those things which are most picturesque make to the Negro the readiest appeal. Red is his favorite color simply because it is the most pronounced of all colors. Goethe's "Faust" can hardly be said to be a play primarily designed for the galleries. One never sees it fail, however, that in any Southern city this play will fill the gallery with the so-called lower class of Negro people, who would never think of going to another play of its class, but different; and the applause never leaves one in doubt as to the reasons for Goethe's popularity. It is the suggestiveness of the love scenes, the red costume of Mephistopheles, the electrical effects, and the rain of fire that give the thrill desired—all pure melodrama of course. "Faust" is a good show as well as a good play.

In some of our communities Negroes are frequently known to "get happy" in church. Now a sermon on the rule of faith or the plan of salvation is never known to awaken such ecstasy. This rather accompanies a vivid portrayal of the beauties of heaven, with the walls of jasper, the angels with palms in their hands, and (*summum bonum!*) the feast of milk and honey. And just here is the dilemma so often faced by the occupants of pulpits in Negro churches. Do the people want scholarly training? Very often the cultured preacher will be inclined to answer in the negative. Do they want rant and shouting? Such a standard fails at once to satisfy the ever-increasing intelligence of the audience itself. The trouble is that the educated minister too often leaves out of account the basic psychology of his audience. That preacher who will ultimately be the most successful with a Negro congregation will be the one who to scholarship and culture can best join brilliant imagination and fervid rhetorical expression. When all of these qualities are brought together in their finest proportion the effect is irresistible.

Gathering up the threads of our discussion so far, we find that there is constant striving on the part of the Negro for beautiful or striking effect, that those things which are most picturesque make the readiest appeal to his nature, and that in the sphere of religion he receives with most appreciation those discourses which are most imaginative in quality. In short, so far as the last point is concerned, it is not too much to assert that the Negro is thrilled not so much by the moral as by the artistic and pictorial elements in religion.

But there is something deeper than the sensuousness of beauty that makes for the possibilities of the Negro in the realm of the arts, and that is the soul of the race. The wail of the old melodies and the plaintive quality that is ever present in the Negro voice are but the reflection of a background of tragedy. No race can rise to the greatest heights of art until it has yearned and suffered. The Russians are a case in point. Such has been their background in oppression and striving that their literature and art are to-day marked by an unmistakable note of power. The same future beckons to the American Negro. There is something very elemental about the heart of the race, something that finds its origin in the African forest, in the sighing of the night-wind, and in the falling of the stars. There is something grim and stern about it all, too, something that speaks of the lash, of the child torn from its mother's bosom, of the dead body riddled with bullets and swinging all night from a limb by the roadside.

So far we have elaborated a theory. Let us not be misunderstood. We do not mean to say that the Negro can not rise to great distinction in any sphere other than the arts. He has already made a noteworthy beginning in pure scholarship and invention; especially have some of the younger men done brilliant work in science. We do mean to say, however, that every race has its peculiar genius, and that, so far as we can at present judge, the Negro, with all his manual labor, is destined to reach his greatest heights in the field of the artistic. But the impulse needs to be watched. Romanticism very soon becomes unhealthy. The Negro has great gifts of voice and ear and soul; but so far much of his talent has not soared above the stage of vaudeville. This is due most largely of course to economic instability. It is the call of patriotism, however, that America should realize that the Negro has peculiar gifts which need all possible cultivation and which will some day add to the glory of the country. Already his music is recognized as the most distinctive that the

United States has yet produced. The possibilities of the race in literature and music, in painting and sculpture, are illimitable.

Along some such lines as these it will be the aim of the following pages to study the literary and artistic achievement of the Negro in the United States. Before we consider individual effort, however, it is worth while to recall folk-lore and folk-music, as in the life and history of the Negro people there has developed an unusual store of customs, superstitions, and tales. Of the writers of the race Charles W. Chesnutt was the first who fully appreciated the value of this material. Its chief literary monument so far has been in the Uncle Remus tales of Joel Chandler Harris. The study of sources and analogues is by no means as simple as one might suppose; it takes one far afield, not only to Africa but even to India and the Continent of Europe. Important as is Negro folk-lore, however, the folk-music is still more so. In recent years this has also been claimed for other countries or nations; but, just as in the folk-lore there is distinctive imagination, so in the music is there a sensuous quality peculiarly the Negro's own. Unlike the English and Scottish popular ballads, the "spirituals" depend for their merit vastly more upon their tunes than upon their words. They are also more affected by nature. A meteoric shower, a thunder-storm, or the dampness of a furrow was sufficient to give birth to a hymn; and there was the freest possible use of figures of speech. As in the ballads, the sentiment becomes universal, and there is a strong tendency toward what has been called incremental repetition; thus, in such a production as "I'm a-Rollin'," after a number of old people had been crooning for a while before a fire, a stanza would at last begin "O brothers, won't you help me?" and the next would be "O sisters, won't you help me?" One soon observes different stages in the development of this music. The first gives that which is simple and elemental, and that takes one to the very heart of the African wilderness, as is the case in "See Fo' an' Twenty Elders on Deir Knees." The second stage exhibits the great class of Afro-American melodies, "Steal Away" being representative. The third shows a blending of Negro music and that of the foster-land, as in "Bright Sparkles in the Churchyard." One may note in passing the influence on the melodies of Baptist and Methodist hymns, also the influence of the Negro temperament on such an American song-writer as Stephen Collins Foster. Those melodies that are most original are generally religious in tone, and sorrowful, as is "Nobody Knows de Trouble I See." Sometimes, however, the note of joy is triumphant, as in "Oh, Give Way, Jordan." No one is able to say just how many of these melodies are in existence, for, while there have been many collections, there is no one that is definitive. Within recent years, with the popular emphasis on "ragtime" and "jazz," there has been a tendency to degrade the Negro "spiritual;" and this has been true even on the part of composers who ought to know better. The integrity of the original melodies should be insisted upon, however, and more and more should the current debasement be discouraged.

For a long time it was supposed that Phillis Wheatley was the first person of African descent in America whose work had appeared in print. Recent investigation, however, has shown that this is not true, and that there was another writer whose first published poem antedated Phillis Wheatley's by a full decade.

Jupiter Hammon was born about 1720 and died about 1800; but these dates are only approximate, as there is no definite evidence on either point. He was first owned by Henry Lloyd, of Lloyd's Neck, Long Island, N. Y. This master died in 1763, leaving him in the part of the inheritance that fell to Joseph, one of his four sons. When Joseph Lloyd died in the course of the Revolutionary War, Hammon passed into the possession of John Lloyd, Jr., a grandson. He was a dutiful and trusted servant, so highly esteemed by the members of the family that they assisted him in placing his verses before the public. In 1761 was printed as a broadside in New York "An Evening Thought. Salvation by Christ, with Penitential Cries: Composed by Jupiter Hammon, a Negro belonging to Mr. Lloyd, of Queen's Village, on Long Island, the 25th of December, 1760.'' The poem consists of eighty-eight lines, and, like all of Hammon's work, emphasizes the religious motive. The second publication was a poetical address to Phillis Wheatley. This was dated Hartford, August 4, 1778, and was also in broadsheet form. It has more personal interest than the first poem, also more strength. Then appeared ''An Essay on the Ten Virgins'' (1779) and ''A Winter Piece'' (Hartford, 1782). This latter production was largely in prose, but contained on the last two pages ''A Poem for Children, with Thoughts on Death.'' ''An Evening's Entertainment,'' written toward the close of the war, has special biographical interest, containing a poetical dialogue entitled ''The Kind Master and the Dutiful Servant.''

Of more abiding significance than any of the verses was ''An Address to the Negroes of the State of New York,'' originally presented to the members of the African Society in the City of New York September 24, 1786, and printed in New York early in 1787. This shows Hammon as feeling it his personal duty to bear slavery with patience but as strongly opposed to the system and as urging that young Negroes be manumitted. The author had to receive editorial assistance before the Address could be issued, but the strong style is his own. There was an immediate reprinting in Philadelphia by order of the Pennsylvania Society for Promoting the Abolition of Slavery, and there was a third edition after Hammon's death. It is worth while to note that in his will dated 1795 John Lloyd, Jr., ordered that certain of his slaves be set free on arriving at the age of twenty-eight; and the Address doubtless had also something to do with the fact that in 1799 the state of New York took formal action looking toward the gradual emancipation of all slaves within her borders. It thus appears that Hammon holds a significant place not only in the literature of the Negro but in the history of the race as well.

II

PHILLIS WHEATLEY

O N one of the slave ships that came to the harbor of Boston in the year 1761 was a little Negro girl of very delicate figure. The vessel on which she arrived came from Senegal. With her dirty face and unkempt hair she must indeed have been a pitiable object in the eyes of would-be purchasers. The hardships of the voyage, however, had given an unusual brightness to the eye of the child, and at least one woman had discernment enough to appreciate her real worth. Mrs. Susannah Wheatley, wife of John Wheatley, a tailor, desired to possess a girl whom she might train to be a special servant for her declining years, as the slaves already in her home were advanced in age and growing feeble. Attracted by the gentle demeanor of the child in question, she bought her, took her home, and gave her the name of Phillis. When the

young slave became known to the world it
was customary for her to use also the name
of the family to which she belonged. She
always spelled her Christian name P-h-i-l-l-i-s.

Phillis Wheatley was born very probably in
1753. The poem on Whitefield published in
1770 said on the title-page that she was seventeen years old. When she came to Boston she
was shedding her front teeth. Her memory of
her childhood in Africa was always vague.
She knew only that her mother *poured out
water before the rising sun*. This was probably
a rite of heathen worship.

Mrs. Wheatley was a woman of unusual re-
finement. Her home was well known to the
people of fashion and culture in Boston, and
King Street in which she lived was then as
noted for its residences as it is now, under the
name of State Street, famous for its commercial
and banking houses. When Phillis entered
the Wheatley home the family consisted of
four persons, Mr. and Mrs. Wheatley, their
son Nathaniel, and their daughter Mary.
Nathaniel and Mary were twins, born May 4,
1743. Mrs. Wheatley was also the mother of
three other children, Sarah, John, and Susan-

nah; but all of these died in early youth.
Mary Wheatley, accordingly, was the only
daughter of the family that Phillis knew to
any extent, and she was eighteen years old
when her mother brought the child to the house,
that is, just a little more than ten years older
than Phillis.

In her new home the girl showed signs of
remarkable talent. Her childish desire for
expression found an outlet in the figures which
she drew with charcoal or chalk on the walls
of the house. Mrs. Wheatley and her daughter
became so interested in the ease with which
she assimilated knowledge that they began to
teach her. Within sixteen months from the
time of her arrival in Boston Phillis was able
to read fluently the most difficult parts of the
Bible. From the first her mistress strove to
cultivate in every possible way her naturally
pious disposition, and diligently gave her instruction in the Scriptures and in morals.
In course of time, thanks especially to the
teaching of Mary Wheatley, the learning of
the young student came to consist of a little
astronomy, some ancient and modern geog-
raphy, a little ancient history, a fair knowledge

of the Bible, and a thoroughly appreciative
acquaintance with the most important Latin
classics, especially the works of Virgil and
Ovid. She was proud of the fact that Terence
was at least of African birth. She became pro-
ficient in grammar, developing a conception of
style from practice rather than from theory.
Pope's translation of Homer was her favorite
English classic. If in the light of twentieth
century opportunity and methods these attainments seem in no wise remarkable, one
must remember the disadvantages under which
not only Phillis Wheatley, but all the women
of her time, labored; and recall that in any
case her attainments would have marked her
as one of the most highly educated young
women in Boston.

While Phillis was trying to make the most
of her time with her studies, she was also seeking to develop herself in other ways. She
had not been studying long before she began
to feel that she too would like to make verses.
Alexander Pope was still an important force
in English literature, and the young student
became his ready pupil. She was about fourteen years old when she seriously began to

cultivate her poetic talent; and one of the
very earliest, and from every standpoint one
of the most interesting of her efforts is the
pathetic little juvenile poem, "On Being
Brought from Africa to America:"

> 'Twas mercy brought me from my pagan land,
> Taught my benighted soul to understand
> That there's a God—that there's a Saviour too:
> Once I redemption neither sought nor knew.
> Some view our sable race with scornful eye—
> "Their colour is a diabolic dye."
> Remember, Christians, Negroes black as Cain
> May be refined, and join th' angelic train.

Meanwhile, the life of Phillis was altogether
different from that of the other slaves of the
household. No hard labor was required of
her, though she did the lighter work, such as
dusting a room or polishing a table. Gradually
she came to be regarded as a daughter and
companion rather than as a slave. As she
wrote poetry, more and more she proved to
have a talent for writing occasional verse.
Whenever any unusual event, such as a death,
occurred in any family of the circle of Mrs.
Wheatley's acquaintance, she would write
lines on the same. She thus came to be re-

garded as "a kind of poet-laureate in the domestic circles of Boston." She was frequently invited to the homes of people to whom Mrs. Wheatley had introduced her, and was regarded with peculiar interest and esteem, on account both of her singular position and her lovable nature. In her own room at home Phillis was specially permitted to have heat and a light, because her constitution was delicate, and in order that she might write down her thoughts as they came to her, rather than trust them to her fickle memory.

Such for some years was the course of the life of Phillis Wheatley. The year 1770 saw the earliest publication of one of her poems. On the first printed page of this edition one might read the following announcement: "A Poem, By Phillis, a Negro Girl, in Boston, On the Death of the Reverend George Whitefield." In the middle of the page is a quaint representation of the dead man in his coffin, on the top of which one might with difficulty decipher, "G. W. Ob. 30 Sept. 1770, Aet. 56." The poem is addressed to the Countess of Huntingdon, whom Whitefield had served as chaplain, and to the orphan children of Georgia whom he had befriended. It takes up in the original less than four pages of large print. It was revised for the 1773 edition of the poems.

In 1771 the first real sorrow of Phillis Wheatley came to her. On January 31st Mary Wheatley left the old home to become the wife of Rev. John Lathrop, pastor of the Second Church in Boston. This year is important for another event. On August 18th "Phillis, the servant of Mr. Wheatley," became a communicant of the Old South Meeting House in Boston. We are informed that "her membership in Old South was an exception to the rule that slaves were not baptized into the church." At that time the church was without a regular minister, though it had lately received the excellent teaching of the Rev. Dr. Joseph Sewell.

This was a troublous time in the history of Boston. Already the storm of the Revolution was gathering. The period was one of vexation on the part of the slaves and their masters as well as on that of the colonies and England. The argument on the side of the slaves was that, as the colonies were still English territory, they were technically free, Lord Mansfield having handed down the decision in 1772 that as soon as a slave touched the soil of England he became free. Certainly Phillis must have been a girl of unusual tact to be able under such conditions to hold so securely the esteem and affection of her many friends.

About this time, as we learn from her correspondence, her health began to fail. Almost all of her letters that are preserved were written to Obour Tanner, a friend living in Newport, R. I. Just when the two young women became acquainted is not known. Obour Tanner survived until the fourth decade of the next century. It was to her, then, still a young woman, that on July 19, 1772, Phillis wrote from Boston as follows:

My Dear Friend,—I received your kind epistle a few days ago; much disappointed to hear that you had not received my answer to your first letter. I have been in a very poor state of health all the past winter and spring, and now reside in the country for the benefit of its more wholesome air. I came to town this morning to spend the Sabbath with my master and mistress. Let me be interested in your prayers that God will bless to me the means used for my recovery, if agreeable to his holy will.

By the spring of 1773 the condition of the health of Phillis was such as to give her friends

much concern. The family physician advised
that she try the air of the sea. As Nathaniel
Wheatley was just then going to England, it
was decided that she should accompany him.
The two sailed in May. The poem, "A Fare-
well to America," is dated May 7, 1773. It
was addressed to "S. W.," that is, Mrs. Wheatley. Before she left America, Phillis was
formally manumitted.

The poem on Whitefield served well as an
introduction to the Countess of Huntingdon.
Through the influence of this noblewoman
Phillis met other ladies, and for the summer the
child of the wilderness was the pet of the
society people of England. Now it was that
a peculiar gift of Phillis Wheatley shone to
advantage. To the recommendations of a
strange history, ability to write verses, and
the influence of kind friends, she added the
accomplishment of brilliant conversation.
Presents were showered upon her. One that
has been preserved is a copy of the magnificent
1770 Glasgow folio edition of "Paradise Lost,"
given to her by Brook Watson, Lord Mayor
of London. This book is now in the library
of Harvard University. At the top of one of

the first pages, in the handwriting of Phillis Wheatley, are these words: "Mr. Brook Watson to Phillis Wheatley, London, July, 1773." At the bottom of the same page, in the handwriting of another, are these words: "This book was given by Brook Watson formerly Lord Mayor of London to Phillis Wheatley & after her death was sold in payment of her husband's debts. It is now presented to the Library of Harvard University at Cambridge, by Dudley L. Pickman of Salem. March, 1824."

Phillis had not arrived in England at the most fashionable season, however. The ladies of the circle of the Countess of Huntingdon desired that she remain long enough to be presented at the court of George III. An accident—the illness of Mrs. Wheatley—prevented the introduction. This lady longed for the presence of her old companion, and Phillis could not be persuaded to delay her return. Before she went back to Boston, however, arrangements were made for the publication of her volume, "Poems on Various Subjects, Religious and Moral," of which more must be said. While the book does not of course contain the later scattered poems, it is the only collection ever brought together by Phillis Wheatley, and the book by which she is known.

The visit to England marked the highest point in the career of the young author. Her piety and faith were now to be put to their severest test, and her noble bearing under hardship and disaster must forever speak to her credit. In much of the sorrow that came to her she was not alone, for the period of the Revolution was one of general distress.

Phillis remained in England barely four months. In October she was back in Boston. That she was little improved may be seen from the letter to Obour Tanner, bearing date the 30th of this month:

I hear of your welfare with pleasure; but this acquaints you that I am at present indisposed by a cold, and since my arrival have been visited by the asthma.

A postscript to this letter reads:

The young man by whom this is handed to you seems to be a very clever man, knows you very well, and is very complaisant and agreeable.

The "young man" was John Peters, afterwards to be her husband.

A great sorrow came to Phillis in the death on March 3, 1774, of her best friend, Mrs. Wheatley, then in her sixty-fifth year. How she felt about this event is best set forth in her own words in a letter addressed to Obour Tanner at Newport under date March 21, 1774:

DEAR OBOUR,—I received your obliging letter enclosed in your Reverend Pastor's and handed me by his son. I have lately met with a great trial in the death of my mistress; let us imagine the loss of a parent, sister or brother, the tenderness of all were united in her. I was a poor little outcast and a stranger when she took me in; not only into her house, but I presently became a sharer in her most tender affections. I was treated by her more like her child than her servant; no opportunity was left unimproved of giving me the best of advice; but in terms how tender! how engaging! This I hope ever to keep in remembrance. Her exemplary life was a greater monitor than all her precepts and instructions; thus we may observe of how much greater force example is than instruction. To alleviate our sorrows we had the satisfaction to see her depart in inexpressible raptures, earnest longings, and impatient thirstings for the *upper* courts of the Lord. Do, my dear friend, remember me and this family in your closet, that this afflicting dispensation may be sanctified to us. I am very sorry to hear that you are indisposed, but hope this will find you in better health. I have been unwell the greater part of the winter, but am much better as the spring approaches. Pray excuse my not writing you so long before, for I have been so busy lately that I could not find leisure. I shall send the 5 books you wrote for, the first convenient opportunity; if you want more they shall be ready for you. I am very affectionately your friend,

PHILLIS WHEATLEY.

After the death of Mrs. Wheatley Phillis seems not to have lived regularly at the old home; at least one of her letters written in 1775 was sent from Providence. For Mr. Wheatley the house must have been a sad one; his daughter was married and living in her own home, his son was living abroad, and his wife was dead. It was in this darkening period of her life, however, that a very pleasant experience came to Phillis Wheatley. This was her reception at the hands of George Washington. In 1775, while the siege of Boston was in progress, she wrote a letter to the distinguished soldier, enclosing a complimentary poem. Washington later replied as follows:

CAMBRIDGE, *Feb. 2, 1776.*

MISS PHILLIS,—Your favor of the 26th of October did not reach my hand till the middle of December. Time enough, you say, to have given an answer ere this. Granted. But a variety of important occurrences continually interposing to distract the mind and to withdraw the attention, I hope, will apologize for the delay and plead my excuse for the seeming, but not real neglect. I thank you most sincerely for your polite notice of me, in the elegant lines you enclosed, and however undeserving I may be of such encomium and panegyric, the style and manner exhibit a striking proof of your poetical talents, in honor of which, and as a tribute justly due to you, I would have published the poem, had I not been apprehensive that while I only meant to give the world this new instance of your genius, I might have incurred the imputation of vanity. This and nothing else determined me not to give it place in the public prints. If you should ever come to Cambridge or near headquarters, I shall be happy to see a person so favored by the muses, and to whom Nature has been so liberal and beneficent in her dispensations.

> I am, with great respect,
> Your obedient humble servant,
> GEORGE WASHINGTON.

Not long afterwards Phillis accepted the invitation of the General and was received in Cambridge with marked courtesy by Washington and his officers.

The Wheatley home was finally broken up by the death of Mr. John Wheatley, March 12, 1778, at the age of seventy-two. After this event Phillis lived for a short time with a friend of Mrs. Wheatley, and then took an apartment and lived by herself. By April she had yielded to the blandishments of John Peters sufficiently to be persuaded to become his wife. This man is variously reported to have been a baker, a barber, a grocer, a doctor, and a lawyer. With all of these professions and occupations, however, he seems not to have possessed the ability to make a living. He wore a wig, sported a cane, and generally felt himself superior to labor. Bereft of old friends as she was, however, sick and lonely, it is not surprising that when love and care seemed thus to present themselves the heart of the woman yielded. It was not long before she realized that she was married to a ne'er-do-well at a time when even an industrious man found it hard to make a living. The course of the Revolutionary War made it more and more difficult for people to secure the bare necessaries of life, and the horrors of Valley Forge were but an aggravation of the general distress. The year was further made memorable by the death of Mary Wheatley, Mrs. Lathrop, on the 24th of September.

When Boston fell into the hands of the British, the inhabitants fled in all directions. Mrs. Peters accompanied her husband to Wil-

mington, Mass., where she suffered much
from poverty. After the evacuation of Boston by
the British troops, she returned thither. A
niece of Mrs. Wheatley, whose son had been
slain in battle, received her under her own
roof. This woman was a widow, was not
wealthy, and kept a little school in order to
support herself. Mrs. Peters and the two
children whose mother she had become remained with her for six weeks. Then Peters
came for his wife, having provided an apartment for her. Just before her departure for
Wilmington, Mrs. Peters entrusted her papers
to a daughter of the lady who received her on
her return from that place. After her death
these were demanded by Peters as the property
of his wife. They were of course promptly
given to him. Some years afterwards he returned to the South, and nothing is known of
what became of the manuscripts.

The conduct of her husband estranged Mrs.
Peters from her old acquaintances, and her
pride kept her from informing them of her
distress. After the war, however, one of Mrs.
Wheatley's relatives hunted her out and found
that her two children were dead, and that a

third that had been born was sick. This
seems to have been in the winter of 1783–84.
Nathaniel Wheatley, who had been living in
London, died in the summer of 1783. In 1784
John Peters suffered imprisonment in jail.
After his liberation he worked as a journeyman
baker, later attempted to practice law, and
finally pretended to be a physician. His wife,
meanwhile, earned her board by drudgery in
a cheap lodging-house on the west side of the
town. Her disease made rapid progress, and
she died December 5, 1784. Her last baby
died and was buried with her. No one of her
old acquaintances seems to have known of her
death. On the Thursday after this event,
however, the following notice appeared in the
Independent Chronicle:

Last Lord's Day, died Mrs. Phillis Peters (formerly
Phillis Wheatley), aged thirty-one, known to the world
by her celebrated miscellaneous poems. Her funeral is
to be this afternoon, at four o'clock, from the house lately
improved by Mr. Todd, nearly opposite Dr. Bulfinch's at
West Boston, where her friends and acquaintances are
desired to attend.

The house referred to was situated on or
near the present site of the Revere House in

Bowdoin Square. The exact site of the grave
of Phillis Wheatley is not known.

At the time when she was most talked about,
Phillis Wheatley was regarded as a prodigy,
appearing as she did at a time when the achievement of the Negro in literature and art was
still negligible. Her vogue, however, was more
than temporary, and the 1793, 1802, and 1816
editions of her poems found ready sale. In
the early years of the last century her verses
were frequently to be found in school readers.
From the first, however, there were those who
discounted her poetry. Thomas Jefferson, for
instance, said that it was beneath the dignity
of criticism. If after 1816 interest in her work
declined, it was greatly revived at the time of
the anti-slavery agitation, when anything in-
dicating unusual capacity on the part of the
Negro was received with eagerness. When
Margaretta Matilda Odell of Jamaica Plain, a
descendant of the Wheatley family, republished
the poems with a memoir in 1834, there was
such a demand for the book that two more
editions were called for within the next three
years. For a variety of reasons, especially an
increasing race-consciousness on the part of

the Negro, interest in her work has greatly increased within the last decade, and as copies of early editions had within recent years become so rare as to be practically inaccessible, the reprint in 1909 of the volume of 1773 by the A. M. E. Book Concern in Philadelphia was especially welcome.

Only two poems written by Phillis Wheatley after her marriage are in existence. These are "Liberty and Peace," and "An Elegy Sacred to the Memory of Dr. Samuel Cooper." Both were published in 1784. Of "Poems on Various Subjects," the following advertisement appeared in the *Boston Gazette* for January 24, 1774:

This Day Published
Adorn'd with an Elegant Engraving of the Author,
(Price 3s. 4d. L. M. Bound,)
POEMS
on various subjects,—Religious and Moral,
By Phillis Wheatley, a Negro Girl.
Sold by Mess's Cox & Berry,
at their Store, in King-Street, Boston.
N. B.—The subscribers are requested to apply for their copies.

The little octavo volume of 124 pages contains 39 poems. One of these, however, must be excluded from the enumeration, as it is simply "A Rebus by I. B.," which serves as the occasion of Phillis Wheatley's poem, the answer to it. Fourteen of the poems are elegiac, and at least six others are occasional. Two are paraphrases from the Bible. We are thus left with sixteen poems to represent the best that Phillis Wheatley had produced by the time she was twenty years old. One of the longest of these is "Niobe in Distress for Her Children Slain by Apollo, from Ovid's Metamorphoses, Book VI, and from a View of the Painting of Mr. Richard Wilson." This poem contains two interesting examples of personification (neither of which seems to be drawn from Ovid), "fate portentous whistling in the air," and "the feather'd vengeance quiv'ring in his hands," though the point might easily be made that these are little more than a part of the pseudo-classic tradition. The poem, "To S. M., a Young African Painter, on seeing his works," was addressed to Scipio Moorhead, a young man who exhibited some talent for drawing and who was a servant of the Rev. John Moorhead of Boston. From the poem we should infer that one of his subjects was the story of Damon and Pythias. Of prime importance are the two or three poems of autobiographical interest. We have already remarked "On Being Brought from Africa to America." In the lines addressed to William, Earl of Dartmouth, the young woman spoke again from her personal experience. Important also in this connection is the poem "On Virtue," with its plea:

> Attend me, Virtue, thro' my youthful years!
> O leave me not to the false joys of time!
> But guide my steps to endless life and bliss.

One would suppose that Phillis Wheatley would make of "An Hymn to Humanity" a fairly strong piece of work. It is typical of the restraint under which she labored that this is one of the most conventional things in the volume. All critics agree, however, that the strongest lines in the book are those entitled "On Imagination." This effort is more sustained than the others, and it is the leading poem that Edmund Clarence Stedman chose to represent Phillis Wheatley in his "Library of American Literature." The following lines are representative of its quality:

> Imagination! Who can sing thy force?
> Or who describe the swiftness of thy course?
> Soaring through air to find the bright abode,
> Th' empyreal palace of the thundering God,
> We on thy pinions can surpass the wind,
> And leave the rolling universe behind:
> From star to star the mental optics rove,
> Measure the skies, and range the realms above;
> There in one view we grasp the mighty whole,
> Or with new worlds amaze th' unbounded soul.

Hardly beyond this is "Liberty and Peace," the best example of the later verse. The poem is too long for inclusion here, but may be found in Duyckinck's "Cyclopedia of American Literature," and Heartman and Schomburg's collected edition of the Poems and Letters.

It is unfortunate that, imitating Pope, Phillis Wheatley more than once fell into his pitfalls. Her diction—"fleecy care," "vital breath," "feather'd race"—is distinctly pseudo-classic. The construction is not always clear; for instance, in the poem, "To Mæcenas," there are three distinct references to Virgil, when grammatically the poetess seems to be speaking of three different men. Then, of course, any young writer working under the influence of Pope and his school would feel a sense of repression. If Phillis Wheatley had come on the scene forty years later, when the romantic writers had given a new tone to English poetry, she would undoubtedly have been much greater. Even as it was, however, she made her mark, and her place in the history of American literature, though not a large one, is secure.

Hers was a great soul. Her ambition knew no bounds, her thirst for knowledge was insatiable, and she triumphed over the most adverse circumstances. A child of the wilderness and a slave, by her grace and culture she satisfied the conventionalities of Boston and of England. Her brilliant conversation was equaled only by her modest demeanor. Everything about her was refined. More and more as one studies her life he becomes aware of her sterling Christian character. In a dark day she caught a glimpse of the eternal light, and it was meet that the first Negro woman in American literature should be one of unerring piety and the highest of literary ideals.

III

THE hundred years after the death of Phillis Wheatley included events of the highest importance for the Negro as for all the people of the United States. For a generation after the Revolution there was reaction from the ideals of Jefferson and Patrick Henry; the cotton-gin was invented, new lands in the South were opened up, and the exploits of Toussaint L'Ouverture and the threat of Gabriel's Insurrection tended to make the actual practice of the slave code more harsh. After 1830, however, things were somewhat different. Garrison founded *The Liberator,* anti-slavery societies became active, and the Negro began to rise to the stature of manhood. At last came John Brown's Raid, the Emancipation Proclamation, and the employment of the Negro soldier at Fort Wagner and Fort Pillow.

It was but natural that in this period there should be much writing about the Negro, and that this writing should have a political cast. It was also but natural that the man who was so much discussed should endeavor in some way to present his own case to the public. Lydia Maria Child and other abolitionists took pride in publishing such things as reflected credit on the race; and there were also the narratives of those persons who had themselves escaped from bondage, outstanding being those of Frederick Douglass, Samuel Ringgold Ward, and Josiah Henson ("Uncle Tom"). All three of these men were prominently before the public just before the Civil War, and we shall later have to refer specially to the oratory of Douglass. Meanwhile, in Philadelphia, Cincinnati, and elsewhere, the Negro began to get an economic foothold; and there were books showing pride in racial achievement, such as William C. Nell's "The Colored Patriots of the American Revolution" and William Wells Brown's "The Black Man: His Antecedents, his Genius, and his Achievements." Brown flourished both before and after the Civil

War. He was a man of talent and traveled
considerably. In addition to books dealing
with Negro history or biography he also
treated racial subjects in a novel, ''Clotel,''
and in a drama, ''The Escape.'' The latter
suffers from an excess of moralizing, but
several times flashes out with the quality of
genuine drama, as when it deals with the
jealousy of a mistress for a favorite slave
and the escape of the latter with her husband.

In 1827, in New York, was begun the pub-
lication of ''Freedom's Journal,'' the first
Negro newspaper in the United States. The
editors were John B. Russwurm and Samuel
E. Cornish. Russwurm was a graduate of
Bowdoin College and was later to become
better known as a governor of Maryland in
Liberia. In 1841 the first Negro magazine
began to appear, this being the organ of the
A. M. E. Church.

In all of this more practical writing, because of its bold and vigorous style, distinction attaches to a booklet appearing in 1829,
David Walker's ''Appeal, in four articles;
together with a Preamble to the Coloured
Citizens of the World, but in particular, and

very expressly, to those of the United States of America.'' This production created the greatest consternation throughout the country. Something of its tone and temper may be seen from the passage in which Walker deals with the plans and proposals of the American Colonization Society:

Here is a demonstrative proof of a plan got up, by a gang of slaveholders, to select the free people of color from among the slaves, that our more miserable brethren may be the better secured in ignorance and wretchedness, to work their farms and dig their mines, and thus go on enriching the Christians with their blood and groans. What our brethren could have been thinking about, who have left their native land and gone away to Africa, I am unable to say. . . . The Americans may say or do as they please, but they have to raise us from the condition of brutes to that of respectable men, and to make a national acknowledgment to us for the wrongs they have inflicted on us. . . . You may doubt it, if you please. I know that thousands will doubt—they think they have us so well secured in wretchedness, to them and their children, that it is impossible for such things to occur. So did the antediluvians doubt Noah, until the day in which the flood came and swept them away. So did the Sodomites doubt, until Lot had got out of the city, and God rained down fire and brimstone from heaven upon them and burnt them up. So did the king of Egypt doubt the very existence of God, saying, *Who is the Lord, that I should let Israel go?* . . . So did the Romans doubt. . . . But they got dreadfully deceived.

Several ambitious spirits attempted verse. Of all who wrote in the second or third quarters of the century, three for one reason or another seem to call for special attention.

The first person to attract much attention after Phillis Wheatley was George Moses Horton, of North Carolina, who was born in 1797 and died about 1880 (or 1883). He was ambitious to learn, was the possessor of unusual literary talent, and in one way or another received instruction from various persons. He very soon began to write verse, all of which was infused with his desire for freedom, and much of which was suggested by the common evangelical hymns, as were the following lines:

> Alas! and am I born for this,
>   To wear this slavish chain?
> Deprived of all created bliss,
>   Through hardship, toil, and pain?
>
> How long have I in bondage lain,
>   And languished to be free!

Alas! and must I still complain,
  Deprived of liberty?

   .   .   .   .   .

Come, Liberty! thou cheerful sound,
  Roll through my ravished ears;
Come, let my grief in joys be drowned,
  And drive away my fears.

Some of Horton's friends became interested in him and desired to help him publish a volume of his poems, so that from the sale of these he might purchase his freedom and go to the new colony of Liberia. The young man became fired with ambition and inspiration. Thrilled by the new hope, he wrote:

'Twas like the salutation of the dove,
Borne on the zephyr through some lonesome grove,
When spring returns, and winter's chill is past,
And vegetation smiles above the blast.

Horton's master, however, demanded for him an exorbitant price, and when "The Hope of Liberty" appeared in 1829 it had nothing of the sale that was hoped for. Disappointed in his great desire, the poet seems to have lost ambition. He became a janitor around the state university at Chapel Hill, executed small commissions for verse from the students, who

treated him kindly, and in later years went
to Philadelphia; but his old dreams had
faded. Several reprintings of his poems were
made, however, and one of these was bound
with the 1838 edition of Phillis Wheatley's
poems.

In 1854 appeared the first edition of
"Poems on Miscellaneous Subjects," by
Frances Ellen Watkins, commonly known as
Mrs. Frances E. W. Harper. Mrs. Harper
was a woman of exceptionally strong personality and could read her poems to advantage. Her verse was very popular, not less
than ten thousand copies of her booklets being sold. It was decidedly lacking in technique, however, and much in the style of Mrs.
Hemans. Mrs. Harper was best when most
simple, as when in writing of children she
said:

> I almost think the angels
>   Who tend life's garden fair,
> Drop down the sweet white blossoms
>   That bloom around us here.

The secret of her popularity was to be seen in
such lines as the following from "Bury Me
in a Free Land":

Make me a grave where'er you will,
In a lowly plain or a lofty hill;
Make it among earth's humblest graves,
But not in a land where men are slaves.

Of the Emancipation Proclamation she wrote:

It shall flash through coming ages,
It shall light the distant years;
And eyes now dim with sorrow
Shall be brighter through their tears.

While Mrs. Harper was still prominently before the public appeared Albery A. Whitman, a Methodist minister, whose "Not a Man and Yet a Man" appeared in 1877. The work of this writer is the most baffling with which this book has to deal. It is diffuse, exhibits many lapses in taste, is uneven metrically, as if done in haste, and shows imitation on every hand. It imitates Whittier, Longfellow, Tennyson, Scott, Byron and Moore. "The Old Sac Village" and "Nanawawa's Suitors" are very evidently "Hiawatha" over again; and "Custer's Last Ride" is simply another version of "The Charge of the Light Brigade." "The Rape of Florida" exhibits the same general characteristics as the earlier poems. And yet, whenever one has about decided that Whitman is not worthy of consideration, he insists on a revision of judgment. The fact is that he shows a decided faculty for brisk narration. This may be seen in "The House of the Aylors." He has, moreover, a romantic lavishness of description that, in spite of all technical faults, still has some degree of merit. The following quotations, taken respectively from "The Mowers" and "The Flight of Leeona," will exemplify both his extravagance and his possibilities in description:

The tall forests swim in a crimson sea,
Out of whose bright depths rising silently,
Great golden spires shoot into the skies,
Among the isles of cloudland high, that rise,
Float, scatter, burst, drift off, and slowly fade,
Deep in the twilight, shade succeeding shade.

·   ·   ·   ·   ·   ·   ·   ·

And now she turns upon a mossy seat,
Where sings a fern-bound stream beneath her feet,
And breathes the orange in the swooning air;
Where in her queenly pride the rose blooms fair,
And sweet geranium waves her scented hair;
There, gazing in the bright face of the stream,
Her thoughts swim onward in a gentle dream.

In "A Dream of Glory" occur the lines:

The fairest blooms are born of humble weeds,
  That faint and perish in the pathless wood;
And out of bitter life grow noble deeds
  To pass unnoticed in the multitude.

Whitman's shortcomings become readily apparent when he attempts sustained work. "The Rape of Florida" is the longest poem yet written by a Negro in America, and also the only attempt by a member of the race to use the elaborate Spenserian stanza throughout a long piece of work. The story is concerned with the capture of the Seminoles in Florida through perfidy and the taking of them away to their new home in the West. It centers around three characters, Palmecho, an old chief, Ewald, his daughter, and Atlassa, a young Seminole who is Ewald's lover. The poem is decidedly diffuse; there is too much subjective description, too little strong characterization. Palmecho, instead of being a stout warrior, is a "chief of peace and kindly deeds." Stanzas of merit, however, occasionally strike the eye. The boat-song forces recognition as genuine poetry:

"Come now, my love, the moon is on the lake;
   Upon the waters is my light canoe;
Come with me, love, and gladsome oars shall make
   A music on the parting wave for you,—
      Come o'er the waters deep and dark and blue;
Come where the lilies in the marge have sprung,
   Come with me, love, for Oh, my love is true!"
This is the song that on the lake was sung,
The boatman sang it over when his heart was young.

In 1890 Whitman brought out an edition of "Not a Man and Yet a Man" and "The Rape of Florida," adding to these a collection of miscellaneous poems, "Drifted Leaves," and in 1901 he published "An Idyl of the South," an epic poem in two parts. It is to be regretted that he did not have the training that comes from the best university education. He had the taste and the talent to benefit from such culture in the greatest degree.

It will thus be seen that, though there was much earnest striving throughout the middle years of the century, practically nothing of abiding literary quality was produced up to the beginning of the last decade. The situation could hardly have been otherwise. Comparatively few persons had received high cultural training, the pressure of making a living was strong, and only here and there did some medium offer encouragement toward expression. Already, however, material was abundant, and it could not be long before a genuine poet would appear to voice the striving of his people.

IV

ORATORS.—DOUGLASS AND WASHINGTON

THE Negro is peculiarly gifted as an orator. To magnificent gifts of voice he adds a fervor of sentiment and an appreciation of the possibilities of a great occasion that are indispensable in the work of one who excels in this field. Greater than any of these things, however, is the romantic quality that finds an outlet in vast reaches of imagery and a singularly figurative power of expression. Only this innate gift of rhetorical expression has accounted for the tremendous effects sometimes realized even by untutored members of the race. Its possibilities under the influences of culture and education are illimitable.

On one occasion Harriet Tubman, famous for her work in the Underground Railroad, was addressing an audience and describing a great battle in the Civil War. "And then," said she, "we saw the lightning, and that

was the guns; and then we heard the thunder,
and that was the big guns; and then we heard
the rain falling, and that was drops of blood
falling; and when we came to git in the craps,
it was dead men that we reaped." * All through
the familiar melodies one finds the pathos and
the poetry of this imagery. Two unusual in-
dividuals, untutored but highly gifted in their
own spheres, in the course of the last century
proved eminently successful by joining this
rhetorical faculty to their native earnestness.
One of these was the anti-slavery speaker,
Sojourner Truth. Tall, majestic, and yet quite
uneducated, this interesting woman sometimes
dazzled her audiences by her sudden turns of
expression. Anecdotes of her quick and start-
ling replies are numberless. The other character was John Jasper, of Richmond, Va.,
famous three decades ago for his "Sun do
move" sermon. Jasper preached not only on
this theme, but also on "Dry bones in the
valley," the glories of the New Jerusalem, and
many similar subjects that have been used by
other preachers, sometimes with hardly less
effect, throughout the South. When one made

*Reported by A. B. Hart, in "Slavery and Abolition," 209.

all discount for the tinsel and the dialect, he
still would have found in the work of John
Jasper much of the power of the true orator.

Other men have joined to this love for
figurative expression the advantages of culture; and a common characteristic, thoroughly
typical of the romantic quality constantly
present, is a fondness for biblical phrase. As
representative might be remarked Robert B.
Elliott, famous for his speech in Congress on
the constitutionality of the Civil Rights Bill;
John Mercer Langston, also distinguished for
many political addresses; M. C. B. Mason, for
years a prominent representative of the Methodist Episcopal Church; and Charles T. Walker,
long the most popular preacher of the Negro
Baptists. A new and telling form of public
speaking, destined to have more and more importance, is that just now best cultivated by
Dr. DuBois, who, with little play of voice or
gesture, but with the earnestness of conviction,
drives home his message with instant effect.

In any consideration of oratory one must
constantly bear in mind, of course, the importance of the spoken word and the personal
equation. At the same time it must be re-

membered that many of the most worthy addresses made by Negroes have not been preserved in accessible form. Again and again, in some remote community, with true eloquence has an untutored preacher brought comfort and inspiration to a struggling people. J. C. Price, for years president of Livingstone College in North Carolina, was one of the truest orators the Negro race ever had, and many who heard him will insist that he was foremost. His name has become in some quarters a synonym for eloquence, and he certainly appeared on many noteworthy occasions with marked effect. His reputation will finally suffer, however, for the reason given, that his speeches are not now generally accessible. Not one is in Mrs. Dunbar's "Masterpieces of Negro Eloquence."

One of the most effective occasional speakers within recent years has been Reverdy C. Ransom, of the A. M. E. Church. In his great moments Mr. Ransom has given the impression of the true orator. He has little humor, is stately and dignified, but bitter in satire and invective. There is, in fact, much in his speaking to remind one of Frederick Douglass. One

of his greatest efforts was that on the occasion
of the celebration of the one hundredth anniversary of the birth of Garrison, in Faneuil
Hall, Boston, December 11, 1905. Said he, in
part:

What kind of Negroes do the American people want?
That they must have the Negro in some relation is no
longer a question of serious debate. What kind of Negroes
do the American people want? Do they want a voteless
Negro in a republic founded upon universal suffrage?
Do they want a Negro who shall not be permitted to
participate in the government which he must support
with his treasure and defend with his blood? Do they
want a Negro who shall consent to be set aside as forming
a distinct industrial class, permitted to rise no higher
than the level of serfs or peasants? Do they want a
Negro who shall accept an inferior social position, not
as a degradation, but as the just operation of the laws of
caste based on color? Do they want a Negro who will
avoid friction between the races by consenting to occupy
the place to which white men may choose to assign him?
What kind of a Negro do the American people want?
. . . Taught by the Declaration of Independence, sustained
by the Constitution of the United States, enlightened
by the education of our schools, this nation can no more
resist the advancing tread of the hosts of the oncoming
blacks than it can bind the stars or halt the resistless
motion of the tide.*

*Quoted from "Masterpieces of Negro Eloquence," 314–5.

Two men, by reason of great natural endowment, a fitting appreciation of great occasions, and the consistency with which they produced their effects, have won an undisputed place in any consideration of American orators. These men were Frederick Douglass and Booker T. Washington.

Frederick Douglass was born in 1817 and lived for ten years as a slave upon a Maryland plantation. Then he was bought by a Baltimore shipbuilder. He learned to read, and, being attracted by "The Lady of the Lake," when he escaped in 1838 and went disguised as a sailor to New Bedford, Mass., he adopted the name *Douglas* (spelling it with two *s's*, however). He lived for several years in New Bedford, being assisted by Garrison in his efforts for an education. In 1841, at an anti-slavery convention in Nantucket, he exhibited such intelligence, and showed himself the possessor of such a remarkable voice, that he was made the agent of the Massachusetts Anti-Slavery Society. He now lectured extensively in England and the United States, and English friends raised £150 to enable him regularly to purchase his freedom. For some years be-

fore the Civil War he lived in Rochester, N. Y.,
where he published a paper, *The North Star*,
and where there is now a public monument
to him. Later in life he became Recorder of
Deeds in the District of Columbia, and then
Minister to Hayti. At the time of his death
in 1895 Douglass had won for himself a place
of unique distinction. Large of heart and of
mind, he was interested in every forward movement for his people; but his charity embraced
all men and all races. His reputation was international, and to-day many of his speeches
are to be found in the standard works on
oratory.

Mr. Chesnutt has admirably summed up
the personal characteristics of the oratory of
Douglass. He tells us that "Douglass possessed, in large measure, the physical equip-
ment most impressive in an orator. He was
a man of magnificent figure, tall, strong, his
head crowned with a mass of hair which made
a striking element of his appearance. He had
deep-set and flashing eyes, a firm, well-moulded
chin, a countenance somewhat severe in re-
pose, but capable of a wide range of expression.
His voice was rich and melodious, and of

carrying power." * Douglass was distinctly dignified, eloquent, and majestic; he could not be funny or witty. Sorrow for the slave, and indignation against the master, gave force to his words, though, in his later years, his oratory became less and less heavy and more refined. He was not always on the popular side, nor was he always exactly logical; thus he incurred much censure for his opposition to the exodus of the Negro from the South in 1879. For half a century, however, he was the outstanding figure of the race in the United States.

Perhaps the greatest speech of his life was that which Douglass made at Rochester on the 5th of July, 1852. His subject was "American Slavery," and he spoke with his strongest invective. The following paragraphs from the introduction will serve to illustrate his fondness for interrogation and biblical phrase:

Pardon me, and allow me to ask, Why am I called upon to speak here to-day? What have I, or those I represent, to do with your national independence? Are the great principles of political freedom and of natural justice embodied in that Declaration of Independence extended to us? And am I, therefore, called upon to bring our humble offering to the national altar, and to

* "Frederick Douglass," 107–8.

confess the benefits, and express devout gratitude for the blessings resulting from your independence to us?

.   .   .   .

By the rivers of Babylon, there we sat down, yea, we wept, when we remembered Zion. We hanged our harps upon the willows in the midst thereof. For there they that carried us away captive required of us a song; and they that had wasted us required of us mirth, saying, Sing us one of the songs of Zion. How shall we sing the Lord's song in a strange land? If I forget thee, O Jerusalem, let my right hand forget her cunning. If I do not remember thee, let my tongue cleave to the roof of my mouth.*

The years and emancipation and the progress of his people in the new day gave a more hopeful tone to some of the later speeches of the orator. In an address on the 7th of December, 1890, he said:

I have seen dark hours in my life, and I have seen the darkness gradually disappearing, and the light gradually increasing. One by one I have seen obstacles removed, errors corrected, prejudices softened, proscriptions relinquished, and my people advancing in all the elements that make up the sum of general welfare. I remember that God reigns in eternity, and that, whatever delays, disappointments, and discouragements may come, truth, justice, liberty, and humanity will prevail.†

* Quoted from Williams, II, 435–6.
† Quoted from Foreword in "In Memoriam: Frederick Douglass."

Booker T. Washington was born about 1858, in Franklin County, Virginia. After the Civil War his mother and stepfather removed to Malden, W. Va., where, when he became large enough, he worked in the salt furnaces and the coal mines. He had always been called Booker, but it was not until he went to a little school at his home and found that he needed a surname that, on the spur of the moment, he adopted *Washington*. In 1872 he worked his way to Hampton Institute, where he paid his expenses by assisting as a janitor. Graduating in 1875, he returned to Malden and taught school for three years. He then attended for a year Wayland Seminary in Washington (now incorporated in Virginia Union University in Richmond), and in 1879 was appointed an instructor at Hampton. In 1881 there came to General Armstrong, principal of Hampton Institute, a call from the little town of Tuskegee, Ala., for someone to organize and become the principal of a normal school which the people wanted to start in that place. He recommended Mr. Washington, who opened the school on the 4th of July in an old church and a little shanty, with an attendance of thirty pupils. In 1895 Mr. Washington came into national prominence by a remarkable speech at the Cotton States Exposition in Atlanta, and after that he interested educators and thinking people generally in the working out of his ideas of practical education. He was the author of several books along lines of industrial education and character-building, and in his later years only one or two other men in America could rival his power to attract and hold great audiences. Harvard University conferred on him the degree of Master of Arts in 1896, and Dartmouth that of Doctor of Laws in 1901. He died in 1915.

In the course of his career Mr. Washington delivered hundreds of addresses on distinguished occasions. He was constantly in demand at colleges and universities, great educational meetings, and gatherings of a civic or public character. His Atlanta speech is famous for the so-called compromise with the white South: "In all things that are purely social we can be as separate as the fingers, yet one as the hand in all things essential to mutual progress." On receiving his degree at Harvard in 1896, he made a speech in which he emphasized the fact that the welfare of the richest and most cultured person in New England was bound up with that of the humblest man in Alabama, and that each man was his brother's keeper. Along somewhat the same line he spoke the next year at the unveiling of the Robert Gould Shaw Monument in Boston. At the Chicago Peace Jubilee in 1898 he reviewed the conduct of the Negro in the wars of the United States, making a powerful plea for justice to a race that had always chosen the better part in the wars of the country. Mr. Washington delivered many addresses, but he never really surpassed the feeling and point and oratorical quality of these early speeches. The following paragraph from the Atlanta speech will illustrate his power of vivid and apt illustration:

A ship lost at sea for many days suddenly sighted a friendly vessel. From the mast of the unfortunate vessel was seen a signal: "Water, water; we die of thirst!" The answer from the friendly vessel at once came back: "Cast down your bucket where you are." A second time the signal, "Water, water; send us water!" ran up from the distressed vessel, and was answered: "Cast down your bucket where you are." And a third and a fourth signal for water was answered: "Cast down your bucket where you are." The captain of the distressed vessel, at last heeding the injunction, cast down his bucket, and it came up full of fresh, sparkling water from the mouth of the Amazon River. To those of my race who depend on bettering their condition in a foreign land, or who underestimate the importance of cultivating friendly relations with the Southern white man, who is their next door neighbor, I would say: "Cast down your bucket where you are"—cast it down in making friends in every manly way of the people of all races by whom we are surrounded.[*]

The power to realize with fine feeling the possibilities of an occasion may be illustrated from the speech at Harvard:

If through me, an humble representative, seven millions of my people in the South might be permitted to send a message to Harvard—Harvard that offered up on death's altar young Shaw, and Russell, and Lowell, and scores of others, that we might have a free and united country—that message would be, Tell them that the sacrifice was not in vain. Tell them that by habits of thrift and economy, by way of the industrial school and college, we are coming up. We are crawling up, working up, yea, bursting up—often through oppression, unjust discrimination and prejudice, but through them all we are coming up, and with proper habits, intelligence, and property, there is no power on earth that can permanently stay our progress.[†]

The eloquence of Douglass differed from that of Washington as does the power of a gifted

[*] Quoted from "Story of My Life and Work," 165–6.
[†] Quoted from "Story of My Life and Work," 210–11.

orator differ from the force of a finished public
speaker. The one was subjective; the other
was objective. Douglass swayed his audience,
and even himself, by the sweep of his passion
and rhetoric; Washington studied every de-
tail and weighed every word, always keeping
in mind the final impression to be made.
Douglass was an idealist, impatient for the
day of perfect fruition; Washington was an
opportunist, making the most of each chance
as it came. The one voiced the sorrows of the
Old Testament, and for the moment produced
the more tremendous effect; the other longed
for the blessing of the New Testament and
spoke with lasting result. Both loved their
people and each in his own way worked as he
could best see the light. By his earnestness
each in his day gained a hearing; by their
sincerity both found a place in the oratory
not only of the Negro but of the world.

V

PAUL LAURENCE DUNBAR

INCOMPARABLY the foremost exponent in verse of the life and character of the Negro people has been Paul Laurence Dunbar. This gifted young poet represented perfectly the lyric and romantic quality of the race, with its moodiness, its abandon, its love of song, and its pathetic irony, and his career has been the inspiration of thousands of the young men and women whose problems he had to face, and whose aspirations he did so much to realize.

Dunbar was born in Dayton, Ohio, June 27, 1872. His parents were uneducated but earnest hard-working people, and throughout his life the love of the poet for his mother was ever a dominating factor. From very early years Dunbar made little attempts at rhyming; but what he afterwards called his first poetical

PAUL LAURENCE DUNBAR

achievement was his recitation of some original verses at a Sunday School Easter celebration when he was thirteen years old. He attended the Steele High School in Dayton, where he was the only Negro student in his class; and by reason of his modest and yet magnetic personality, he became very popular with his schoolmates. In his second year he became a member of the literary society of the school, afterwards became president of the same, as well as editor of *The High School Times*, a monthly student publication, and on his completion of the course in 1891 he composed the song for his class. Somewhat irregularly for the next two or three years Dunbar continued his studies, but he never had the advantage of a regular college education. On leaving the high school, after vainly seeking for something better, he accepted a position as elevator boy, working for four dollars a week. In 1893, at the World's Columbian Exposition in Chicago, he was given a position by Frederick Douglass, who was in charge of the exhibit from Hayti. "Oak and Ivy" appeared in 1893, and "Majors and Minors" in 1895. These little books were privately printed; Dunbar had to assume

full responsibility for selling them, and not
unnaturally he had many bitter hours of dis-
couragement. Asking people to buy his verses
grated on his sensitive nature, and he once
declared to a friend that he would never sell
another book. Sometimes, however, he suc-
ceeded beyond his highest hopes, and gradually, with the assistance of friends, chief among
whom was Dr. H. A. Tobey, of Toledo, the
young poet came into notice as a reader of his
verses. William Dean Howells wrote a full-
page review of his poems in the issue of *Harper's Weekly* that contained an account of William McKinley's first nomination for the presi-
dency. Dunbar was now fairly launched upon
his larger fame, and "Lyrics of Lowly Life,"
published by Dodd, Mead & Co. in 1896, introduced him to the wider reading public.
This book is deservedly the poet's best known.
It contained the richest work of his youth
and was really never surpassed. In 1897 Dunbar enhanced his reputation as a reader of
his own poems by a visit to England. About
this time he was very busy, writing numerous
poems and magazine articles, and meeting
with a success that was so much greater than

that of most of the poets of the day that it became a vogue. In October, 1897, through the influence of Robert G. Ingersoll, he secured employment as an assistant in the reading room of the Library of Congress, Washington; but he gave up this position after a year, for the confinement and his late work at night on his own account were making rapid inroads upon his health. On March 6, 1898, Dunbar was married to Alice Ruth Moore, of New Orleans, who also had become prominent as a writer. Early in 1899 he went South, visiting Tuskegee and other schools, and giving many readings. Later in the same year he went to Colorado in a vain search for health. Books were now appearing in rapid succession, short story collections and novels as well as poems. "The Uncalled," written in London, reflected the poet's thought of entering the ministry. It was followed by "The Love of Landry," a Colorado story; "The Fanatics," and "The Sport of the Gods." Collections of short stories were, "Folks from Dixie," "The Strength of Gideon," "In Old Plantation Days," and "The Heart of Happy Hollow." Volumes of verse were "Lyrics of the Hearthside,"

"Lyrics of Love and Laughter," "Lyrics of Sunshine and Shadow," as well as several specially illustrated volumes. Dunbar bought a home in Dayton, where he lived with his mother. His last years were a record of sincere friendships and a losing fight against disease. He died February 9, 1906. He was only thirty-three, but he "had existed millions of years."

Unless his novels are considered as forming a distinct class, Dunbar's work falls naturally into three divisions: the poems in classic English, those in dialect, and the stories in prose. It was his work in the Negro dialect that was his distinct contribution to American literature. That this was not his desire may be seen from the eight lines entitled, "The Poet," in which he longed for success in the singing of his "deeper notes" and spoke of his dialect as "a jingle in a broken tongue." Any criticism of Dunbar's classic English verse will have to reckon with the following poems: "Ere Sleep Comes Down to Soothe the Weary Eyes," "The Poet and His Song," "Life," "Promise and Fulfillment," "Ships That Pass in the Night," and "October." In the pure

flow of lyrical verse the poet rarely surpassed
his early lines:*

> Ere sleep comes down to soothe the weary eyes,
>   How questioneth the soul that other soul—
> The inner sense which neither cheats nor lies,
>   But self exposes unto self, a scroll
> Full writ with all life's acts unwise or wise,
>   In characters indelible and known;
> So, trembling with the shock of sad surprise,
>   The soul doth view its awful self alone,
> Ere sleep comes down to soothe the weary eyes.

"The Poet and his Song" is also distinguished
for its simplicity and its lyric quality:

> A song is but a little thing,
> And yet what joy it is to sing!
> In hours of toil it gives me zest,
> And when at eve I long for rest;
> When cows come home along the bars,
>   And in the fold I hear the bell,
> As night, the Shepherd, herds his stars,
>   I sing my song, and all is well.
>
> . . . . . .
>
> Sometimes the sun, unkindly hot,
> My garden makes a desert spot;

* As stated in the Preface, we are under obligations to
Dodd, Mead & Co. for permission to use the quotations from
Dunbar. These are covered by copyright by this firm, as
follows: "Ere Sleep Comes Down to Soothe the Weary Eyes,"
"The Poet and his Song," and "Life," 1896; Lullaby," 1899;
and "Compensation," 1905.

> Sometimes a blight upon the tree
> Takes all the fruit away from me;
> And then with throes of bitter pain
>   Rebellious passions rise and swell;
> But life is more than fruit or grain,
>   And so I sing, and all is well.

The two stanzas entitled "Life" have probably been quoted more than any other lines written by the poet:

> A crust of bread and a corner to sleep in,
> A minute to smile and an hour to weep in,
> A pint of joy to a peck of trouble,
> And never a laugh but the moans come double;
>   And that is life.

> A crust and a corner that love makes precious,
> With a smile to warm and the tears to refresh us;
> And joy seems sweeter when cares come after,
> And a moan is the finest of foils for laughter;
>   And that is life.

"Promise and Fulfillment" was especially admired by Mrs. Minnie Maddern Fiske, who frequently recited it with never-failing applause. Of the poet's own reading of "Ships that Pass in the Night" on one occasion, Brand Whitlock wrote: "That last evening he recited—oh! what a voice he had—his 'Ships that Pass in the Night.' I can hear him now and see the expression on his fine face as he said, 'Passing! Passing!' It was prophetic."

Other pieces, no more distinguished in poetic quality, are of special biographical interest. "Robert Gould Shaw" was the expression of pessimism as to the Negro's future in America. "To Louise" was addressed to the young daughter of Dr. Tobey, who, on one occasion, when the poet was greatly depressed, in the simple way of a child cheered him by her gift of a rose. "The Monk's Walk" reflects the poet's thought of being a preacher. Finally, there is the swan song, "Compensation," contributed to *Lippincott's*, eight exquisite lines:

> Because I had loved so deeply,
>   Because I had loved so long,
> God in his great compassion
>   Gave me the gift of song.
>
> Because I have loved so vainly,
>   And sung with such faltering breath,
> The Master in infinite mercy
>   Offers the boon of Death.

The dialect poems suffer by quotation, being artistic primarily as wholes. Of these, by common consent, the masterpiece is "When Malindy Sings," a poem inspired by the singing of the poet's mother. Other pieces in dialect that have proved unusually successful, especially as readings, are "The Rivals," "A Coquette Conquered," "The Ol' Tunes," "A Corn-Song," "When de Co'n Pone's Hot," "How Lucy Backslid," "The Party," "At Candle-Lightin' Time," "Angelina," "Whistling Sam," "Two Little Boots," and "The Old Front Gate." Almost all of these poems represent the true humorist's blending of humor and pathos, and all of them exemplify the delicate and sympathetic irony of which Dunbar was such a master. As representative of the dialect verse at its best, attention might be called to a little poem that was included in the illustrated volume, "Candle-Lightin' Time," but that, strangely enough, was omitted from both of the larger editions of the poems, very probably because the title, "Lullaby," was used more than once by the poet:

> Kiver up yo' haid, my little lady,
>   Hyeah de win' a-blowin' out o' do's,
> Don' you kick, ner projick wid de comfo't,
>   Less'n fros 'll bite yo' little toes.

Shut yo' eyes, an' snuggle up to mammy;
  Gi' me bofe yo' han's, I hol' 'em tight;
Don' you be afeard, an' 'mence to trimble
  Des ez soon ez I blows out de light.

Angels is a-mindin' you, my baby,
  Keepin' off de Bad Man in de night.
Whut de use o' bein' skeered o' nuffin'?
  You don' fink de da'kness gwine to bite?
Whut de crackin' soun' you hyeah erroun' you?—
  Lawsy, chile, you tickles me to def!—
Dat's de man what brings de fros', a-paintin'
  Picters on de winder wid his bref.

Mammy ain' afeard, you hyeah huh laughin'?
  Go 'way, Mistah Fros', you can't come in;
Baby ain' erceivin' folks dis evenin',
  Reckon dat you 'll have to call ag'in.
Curl yo' little toes up so, my 'possum—
  Umph, but you's a cunnin' one fu' true!—
Go to sleep, de angels is a-watchin',
  An' yo' mammy's mindin' of you, too.

The short stories of Dunbar would have
been sufficient to make his reputation, even
if he had not written his poems. One of the
best technically is "Jimsella," from the "Folks
from Dixie" volume. This story exhibits the
pathos of the life of unskilled Negroes in the
North, and the leading of a little child. In
the sureness with which it moves to its con-

clusion it is a beautiful work of art. "A Family
Feud" shows the influence of an old servant
in a wealthy Kentucky family. In similar
vein is "Aunt Tempe's Triumph." "The
Walls of Jericho" is an exposure of the methods
of a sensational preacher. Generally these
stories attempt no keen satire, but only a
faithful portrayal of conditions as they are,
or, in most cases, as they were in ante-bellum
days. Dunbar's novels are generally weaker
than his short stories, though "The Sport of
the Gods," because of its study of a definite
phase of life, rises above the others. Nor are
his occasional articles especially strong. He
was eminently a lyric poet. By his graceful
and beautiful verse it is that he has won a
distinct place in the history of American literature.

By his genius Paul Laurence Dunbar attracted the attention of the great, the wise,
and the good. His bookcase contained many
autograph copies of the works of distinguished
contemporaries. The similarity of his position
in American literature to that of Burns in
English has frequently been pointed out. In
our own time he most readily invites comparison

with James Whitcomb Riley. The writings of both men are distinguished by infinite tenderness and pathos. But above all worldly fame, above even the expression of a struggling people's heart, was the poet's own striving for the unattainable. There was something heroic about him withal, something that links him with Keats, or, in this latter day, with Rupert Brooke and Alan Seeger. He yearned for love, and the world rushed on; then he smiled at death and was universally loved.

VI

CHARLES W. CHESNUTT

CHARLES WADDELL CHESNUTT, the best known novelist and short story writer of the race, was born in Cleveland, Ohio, June 20, 1858. At the age of sixteen he began to teach in the public schools of North Carolina, from which state his parents had gone to Cleveland; and at the age of twenty-three he became principal of the State Normal School at Fayetteville. In 1883 he left the South, engaging for a short while in newspaper work in New York City, but going soon to Cleveland, where he worked as a stenographer. He was admitted to the bar in 1887.

While in North Carolina Mr. Chesnutt studied to good purpose the dialect, manners, and superstitions of the Negro people of the state. In 1887 he began in the *Atlantic Monthly* the series of stories which was afterwards brought together in the volume entitled, "The

CHARLES W. CHESNUTT

Conjure Woman." This book was published by the Houghton Mifflin Co., the firm which published also Mr. Chesnutt's other collection of stories and the first two of his three novels. "The Wife of his Youth, and Other Stories of the Color-Line" appeared in 1899. In the same year appeared a compact biography of Frederick Douglass, a contribution to the Beacon Biographies of Eminent Americans. Three novels have since appeared, as follows: "The House Behind the Cedars" (1900); "The Marrow of Tradition" (1901); and "The Colonel's Dream"(1905).

Mr. Chesnutt's short stories are not all of the same degree of excellence, but the best ones show that he is fully master of the short story as a literary form. One of the best technically is "The Bouquet." This is a story of the devotion of a little Negro girl to her white teacher, and shows clearly how the force of Southern prejudice might forbid the expression of simple love not only in a representative home, but even when the object of the devotion is borne to the cemetery. "The Sheriff's Children" is a tragic tale of the relations of a white father with his illegitimate colored son.

Most famous of all these stories, however, is
"The Wife of his Youth," a simple work of
art of great intensity. It is a tale of a very
fair colored man who, just before the Civil
War, by the aid of his Negro wife, makes his
way from slavery in Missouri to freedom in a
Northern city, Groveland [Cleveland?]. After
the years have brought to him business success and culture, and he has become the
acknowledged leader of his social circle and the
prospective husband of a very attractive young
widow, his wife suddenly appears on the scene.
The story ends with Mr. Ryder's acknowl-
edging before a company of guests the wife of
his youth. Such stories as these, each setting
forth a certain problem and working it out to
its logical conclusion, reflect great credit upon
the literary skill of the writer.

Of the novels, "The House Behind the
Cedars" is commonly given first place. In
the story of the heroine, Rena Walden, are
treated some of the most subtle and searching questions raised by the color-line. Rena
is sought in love by three men, George Tryon,
a white man, whose love fails when put to
the test; Jeff Wain, a coarse and brutal mu-

latto, and Frank Fowler, a devoted young
Negro, who makes every sacrifice demanded
by love. The novel, especially in its last
pages, moves with an intensity that is an unmistakable sign of power. It is Mr. Chesnutt's most sustained treatment of the subject
for which he has become best known, that is,
the delicate and tragic situation of those who
live on the border-line of the races; and it is
the best work of fiction yet written by a member of the race in America. In "The Marrow
of Tradition" the main theme is the relations
of two women, one white and one colored,
whose father, the same white man, had in
time been married to the mother of each.
The novel touches upon almost every phase
of the Negro Problem. It is a powerful plea,
but perhaps too much a novel of purpose to
satisfy the highest standards of art. The
Wellington of the story is very evidently Wilmington, N. C., and the book was written
immediately after the race troubles in that city
in 1898. "The Colonel's Dream" is a sad
story of the failure of high ideals. Colonel
Henry French is a man who, born in the South,
achieves success in New York and returns to

his old home for a little vacation, only to find himself face to face with all the problems that one meets in a backward Southern town. "He dreamed of a regenerated South, filled with thriving industries, and thronged with a prosperous and happy people, where every man, having enough for his needs, was willing that every other man should have the same; where law and order should prevail unquestioned, and where every man could enter, through the golden door of hope, the field of opportunity, where lay the prizes of life, which all might have an equal chance to win or lose." Becoming interested in the injustice visited upon the Negroes in the courts, and in the employment of white children in the cotton-mills, Colonel French encounters opposition to his benevolent plans, opposition which finally sends him back to New York defeated. Mr. Chesnutt writes in simple, clear English, and his methods might well be studied by younger writers who desire to treat, in the guise of fiction, the many searching questions that one meets to-day in the life of the South. In 1928 he was awarded the Spingarn Medal for distinguished achievement. This is an honor that will more than once be mentioned in these pages. It arose from the fact that in 1914 Dr. Joel E. Spingarn began the annual offer of a gold medal of the value of one hundred dollars to be awarded to that Negro man or woman who, by his or her individual achievement as judged by a committee, shall have reflected most credit upon the race in any honorable field of endeavor.

VII

WILLIAM EDWARD BURGHARDT DUBOIS was born February 23, 1868, at Great Barrington, Mass. He received the degree of Bachelor of Arts at Fisk University in 1888, the same degree at Harvard in 1890, that of Master of Arts at Harvard in 1891, and, after a season of study at the University of Berlin, received also the degree of Doctor of Philosophy at Harvard in 1895, his thesis being "The Suppression of the African Slave-Trade to the United States of America." Dr. DuBois taught for a brief period at Wilberforce University, and was also for a time an assistant and fellow in Sociology at the University of Pennsylvania, producing in 1899 his study "The Philadelphia Negro." In 1896 he accepted the professorship of History and Economics at Atlanta University. For a number of years he was the moving

W. E. BURGHARDT DU BOIS

spirit of the Atlanta Conference, and by the Studies of Negro Problems which he annually edited in this connection he became recognized as one of the outstanding sociologists of the day. In 1910 he left Atlanta to go to New York as director of Publicity and Research for the National Association for the Advancement of Colored People. He has made various investigations, sometimes for the national Government, and has contributed numerous articles to leading magazines.

Aside from his more technical studies Dr. DuBois has written five books which call for consideration in a review of Negro literature. Of these one is a biography, two are novels, and two are collections of essays and sketches. In 1909 appeared "John Brown," a contribution to the series of American Crisis Biographies. The subject was one well adapted to treatment at the hands of the author, and in the last chapter, "The Legacy of John Brown," he showed that his hero had a message for twentieth century America, this: "The cost of liberty is less than the price of repression."

The two novels not unnaturally reflect the

public work of Dr. DuBois. "The Quest of
the Silver Fleece" (1911) has three main
themes: the economic position of the Negro
agricultural laborer, the subsidizing of a certain kind of Negro school, and Negro life and
society in the city of Washington. The book
employs a big theme in its portrayal of the
power of King Cotton in the life of both the
high and the lowly in the South; but its tone
is frequently one of satire, the chief characters are hardly plausibly developed, and on
the whole the work offered little that could
add to the already established reputation of
the author. Nearly two decades later appeared "Dark Princess" (1928), a work more
intense even if not better organized. In this
the real theme is the furious conflict that
rages in the hearts of Negro men. To some
extent the book is episodic and kaleidoscopic
in manner; nevertheless certain characters
stand out clearly. Matthew Towns passes
through suffering to a deeper understanding
of the tragedy of his people. "We come out
of the depths," he says, "the blood and mud
of battle. And from just such depths, I take
it, came most of the worth while things in this

old world." Then there is Perigua, the revolutionist, who with something of irony blows himself up with the dynamite intended for others; and Sara Andrews, the hard, clever woman of the world, who cares nothing for those less fortunate, perfectly satisfied if she at least is smug and comfortable.

The other two books give the author's reaction to the seething cauldron in which he has lived most of his life. In 1903 fourteen essays, some of which had appeared in such magazines as the *Atlantic* and *The World's Work,* were brought together in a volume entitled "The Souls of Black Folk." The remarkable style of this book has made it the most important work in classic English yet written by a Negro. Where merit is so even and the standard of performance so high, one hesitates to choose that which is best. "The Dawn of Freedom" is a study of the Freedmen's Bureau; "Mr. Booker T. Washington and Others" is a frank criticism of the late orator and leader; "The Meaning of Progress" is a story of life in Tennessee, told with infinite pathos by one who has been the country schoolmaster; "The Training of

Black Men'' is a plea for a liberally educated
leadership, while ''The Quest of the Golden
Fleece,'' like one or two related essays, is a
faithful portrayal of life in the black belt.
The book as a whole is a powerful plea for
justice and the liberty of citizenship; nor can
a certain note of pessimism that runs through
it detract from its literary quality. Not quite
so successful was the later book, ''Darkwater'' (1920). This was written at white
heat about the close of the war, when one
could not overlook injustice on the part of
even the Government of the country; and the
writing has a tone just a little too strident
for the most felicitous effect.

It appears then that after the lapse of
years ''The Souls of Black Folk'' remains
the author's best work. This it is that shows
his style at his best. That style is marked by
all the arts of rhetoric—by strong antithesis,
frequent allusion, liquid and alliterative effects, and poetic suggestiveness. The color-
line is the ''Veil,'' the familiar melodies the
''Sorrow Songs.'' The following paragraphs
will illustrate the qualities that have just
been remarked:

I have seen a land right merry with the sun, where children sing, and rolling hills lie like passioned women wanton with harvest. And there in the King's Highway sat and sits a figure veiled and bowed, by which the traveler's footsteps hasten as they go. On the tainted air broods fear. Three centuries' thought has been the raising and unveiling of that bowed human heart, and now behold a century new for the duty and the deed. The problem of the Twentieth Century is the problem of the color-line.

. . . .

I sit with Shakespeare and he winces not. Across the color-line I move arm in arm with Balzac and Dumas, where smiling men and welcoming women glide in gilded halls. From out the caves of evening that swing between the strong-limbed earth and the tracery of the stars, I summon Aristotle and Aurelius and what soul I will, and they all come graciously with no scorn nor condescension. So, wed with Truth, I dwell above the Veil. Is this the life you grudge us, O knightly America? Is this the life you long to change into the dull red hideousness of Georgia? Are you so afraid lest peering from this high Pisgah, between Philistine and Amalekite, we sight the Promised Land?

. . . .

My journey was done, and behind me lay hill and dale, and Life and Death. How shall man measure Progress there where the dark-faced Josie lies? How many heartfuls of sorrow shall balance a bushel of wheat? How hard a thing is life to the lowly, and yet how human and real! And all this life and love and strife and failure—is it the twilight of nightfall or the flush of some faint-dawning day?

Thus sadly musing, I rode to Nashville in the Jim Crow Car.

W. E. Burghardt DuBois combines in unusual degree the temper of the scholar and the romanticism of the Negro race. Forced by the pressure of circumstance, gradually he was led from the congenial retreat of the student into the open arena of social struggle. For more than two decades now he has striven to interpret the desires and the aspirations of his people. He has traveled thousands of miles and delivered hundreds of addresses, and all of this service has been very necessary. One can not help recalling, however, that in a strictly literary way the best work he has done was that which he did on a hill in Atlanta thirty years ago. Then it was that, with all the ringing of bells and hurrying to and fro, he did yeoman service as a teacher. Then too it was that he daily inspired and was inspired by eager, earnest youth.

VIII

PROMINENT for some years, first as poet and then as critic, has been William Stanley Braithwaite, of Boston. The work of this author belongs not so much to Negro literature as to American literature in the large, and he has encouraged and inspired a host of other writers. With singleness of purpose he has given himself to books and the book world, and it is by this devotion that he has won the distinct success that he has achieved.

In 1904 Mr. Braithwaite published a small volume of poems entitled "Lyrics of Life and Love." This was followed four years later by "The House of Falling Leaves." Within recent years, however, he has given little time to his own verse, becoming more and more distinguished as a critic of American poetry. For several years he has been a valued con-

tributor to *The Boston Evening Transcript,*
and he has had verse or critical essays in
The Forum, the *Century, Scribner's,* and the
Atlantic. He has collected and edited "The
Book of Elizabethan Verse," "The Book of
Georgian Verse," and "The Book of Restoration Verse;" he has published the "Anthology of Magazine Verse" for each year
since 1913, also "The Golden Treasury of
Magazine Verse;" and, while editor of the
Poetry Review in 1916, he projected a series
of Contemporary American Poets. In 1917
he brought together in a volume, "The Poetic
Year," a special series of articles which he
had contributed to the *Transcript.* The aim
of this was, in the form of conversations
among a small group of friends, to whom
fanciful and suggestive Greek names had
been given, to discuss the poetry that had
appeared in 1916. After the war appeared
"Victory: Celebrated by Thirty-eight American Poets" and "The Story of the Great
War" for young people. In 1918 Mr. Braithwaite was awarded the Spingarn Medal.

In a review of this writer's poetry we have
to consider especially the two collections,

WILLIAM STANLEY BRAITHWAITE

"Lyrics of Life and Love," and "The House of Falling Leaves," and the poems that have more recently appeared in the *Atlantic, Scribner's,* and other magazines. It is to be hoped that before very long he will publish a new edition of his poems. The earlier volumes are out of print, and a new book could contain the best of them, as well as what has appeared more recently. "Lyrics of Life and Love" embodied the best of the poet's early work. The little book contains eighty pages, and no one of the lyrics takes up more than two pages, twenty in fact being exactly eight lines in length. This appearance of fragility, however, is a little deceptive. While Keats and Shelley are constantly evident as the models in technique, the yearning of more than one lyric reflects the deeper romantic temper. The bravado and the tenderness of the old poets are evident again in the two Christmas pieces, "Holly Berry and Mistletoe," and "Yule-Song: A Memory":

> The trees are bare, wild flies the snow,
>   Hearths are glowing, hearts are merry—
> High in the air is the Mistletoe,
>   Over the door is the Holly Berry.

Never have care how the winds may blow,
　　Never confess the revel grows weary—
Yule is the time of the Mistletoe,
　　Yule is the time of the Holly Berry.

　　.　　.　　.　　.　　.　　.　　.

December comes, snows come,
　　Comes the wintry weather;
Faces from away come—
　　Hearts must be together.
　　　　Down the stair-steps of the hours
　　　　Yule leaps the hills and towers—
　　Fill the bowl and hang the holly,
　　Let the times be jolly.

"The Watchers" is in the spirit of Kingsley's "The Three Fishers":

Two women on the lone wet strand—
　　(*The wind's out with a will to roam*)
The waves wage war on rocks and sand,
　　(*And a ship is long due home.*)

The sea sprays in the women's eyes—
　　(*Hearts can writhe like the sea's wild foam*)
Lower descend the tempestuous skies,
　　(*For the wind's out with a will to roam.*)

"O daughter, thine eyes be better than mine,"
　　(*The waves ascend high on yonder dome*)
"North or South is there never a sign?"
　　(*And a ship is long due home.*)

They watched there all the long night through—
  (*The wind's out with a will to roam*)
Wind and rain and sorrow for two—
  (*And heaven on the long reach home.*)

The second volume marked a decided advance in technique. When we remember also the Pre-Raphaelite spirit, with its love of rhythm and imagery, we are not surprised to find here an appreciation "To Dante Gabriel Rossetti." Especially has the poet made progress in the handling of the sonnet, as may be seen in the following:

My thoughts go marching like an armèd host
  Out of the city of silence, guns and cars;
Troop after troop across my dreams they post
  To the invasion of the wind and stars.
O brave array of youth's untamed desire!
  With thy bold, dauntless captain Hope to lead
His raw recruits to Fate's opposing fire,
  And up the walls of Circumstance to bleed.
How fares the expedition in the end?
  When this my heart shall have old age for king
And to the wars no further troop can send,
  What final message will the arm'stice bring?
The host gone forth in youth the world to meet,
In age returns—in victory or defeat?

Then there is the epilogue with its heart-cry:

Lord of the mystic star-blown gleams
Whose sweet compassion lifts my dreams;
Lord of life in the lips of the rose
That kiss desire; whence Beauty grows;
Lord of the power inviolate
That keeps immune thy seas from fate,

. . . .

Lord, Very God of these works of thine,
Hear me, I beseech thee, most divine!

Within very recent years Mr. Braithwaite
has attracted unusual attention among the
discerning by a new note of mysticism that
has crept into his verse. This was first observed in "Sandy Star," that appeared in
the *Atlantic* (July, 1909):

No more from out the sunset,
  No more across the foam,
No more across the windy hills
  Will Sandy Star come home.

He went away to search it,
  With a curse upon his tongue,
And in his hands the staff of life
  Made music as it swung.

I wonder if he found it,
  And knows the mystery now:
Our Sandy Star who went away
  With the secret on his brow.

The same note is in "The Mystery" (or "The Way," as the poet prefers to call it) that appeared in *Scribner's* (October, 1915):

> He could not tell the way he came
>   Because his chart was lost:
> Yet all his way was paved with flame
>   From the bourne he crossed.
>
> He did not know the way to go,
>   Because he had no map:
> He followed where the winds blow,—
>   And the April sap.
>
> He never knew upon his brow
>   The secret that he bore—
> And laughs away the mystery now
>   The dark's at his door.

Mr. Braithwaite has done well. He has consistently kept before him his vision, and after years of hard work his position is now one of unique distinction. A few years ago a special reception was accorded him in New York by the authors of America, and in an editorial of November 30, 1915, the *Transcript* said: "He has helped poetry to readers as well as to poets. One is guilty of no extravagance in saying that the poets we have —and they may take their place with their peers in any country—and the gathering deference we pay them, are created largely out of the stubborn, self-effacing enthusiasm of this one man. In a sense their distinction is his own. In a sense he has himself written their poetry. Very much by his toil they may write and be read. Not one of them will ever write a finer poem than Braithwaite himself has lived already.''

IX

WITH a varied career, including service as teacher, author, and publicist, James Weldon Johnson has steadily forged to the front. To-day he is in letters one of the most prominent men of the race in the United States.

Mr. Johnson was born in Jacksonville, Fla., in 1871. His father was a minister and his mother was fond of music. In 1894 he was graduated at Atlanta University; ten years later this institution conferred upon him the degree of Master of Arts; he continued his studies at Columbia; and he later received the degree of Doctor of Letters from Talladega College and Howard University. For seven years after graduating from college he was principal of a public school in Jacksonville, and, with the tact that was later to be one of his outstanding qualities, he gradually raised the status of an institution that had been doing only grammar grade work to that of a full-fledged high school. Meanwhile he studied law, in course of time being admitted to the bar in Florida. While still in Jacksonville also, he began with his brother, Rosamond Johnson, the composer, that collaboration in song-making which within the next few years was to prove so successful. In 1900 one wrote the words and the other the music for "Lift Ev'ry Voice and Sing," now widely known as the Negro National Anthem. This was originally composed for a group of school-children preparing for a Lincoln's birthday exercise, but its noble words and swelling music made it deservedly popular, and it is now regularly sung in Negro schools and colleges throughout the country. In 1901 the brothers launched forth upon the great adventure of their lives, and removed to New York. It was the day of Ernest Hogan, and Williams and Walker in musical comedy; and the Cole and Johnson company became one of the best known of the decade. The writing of the words for popular songs was fairly lucrative, but after

JAMES WELDON JOHNSON

a while it palled upon a man with aspirations for higher things, and in 1906 Mr. Johnson accepted the post of United States consul to Puerto Cabello, Venezuela. Here he remained until 1909, when he was transferred to a more important post at Corinto, Nicaragua, where he served until 1912. As a consul he saw three revolutions, one in Venezuela and two in Nicaragua, and in general his work for the Government gave him valuable experience and broader contact. Far from New York also, with all the coming and going of ships and tourists, he still had time to find his soul. Returning home he found a new life awaiting him, first as field secretary and then as secretary of the National Association for the Advancement of Colored People. In 1915 he made for the Metropolitan Opera the English translation of the Spanish opera "Goyescas," by Granados and Periquet; and in 1916, while connected with *The New York Age,* he won a third prize of two hundred dollars in a competition opened by *The Public Ledger,* of Philadelphia, to editorial writers throughout the country. His poem, "The Young Warrior," set to stirring music by Harry T. Burleigh, was sung in the course of the war by Mr. Amato, of the Metropolitan Opera, with tremendous effect; and the Italian version was soon popular throughout Italy. In 1920 he went to Hayti to investigate conditions under the American occupation. In 1925 he was awarded the Spingarn Medal for his service "as diplomat, author, and publicist."

Mr. Johnson's first formal publication, "Autobiography of an Ex-Colored Man," was published anonymously in 1912, but in 1927 was given new issue with the author's name. The method of the book is primarily that of fiction, but the writer draws upon his own experience as freely as he chooses. So doing he is able to interpret without any restriction the life of which he has been a part. In the career of the central figure who, born in Georgia, attends school in Connecticut, and later looks large-eyed upon the world, the book touches upon practically every phase of the so-called Negro problem. While it is as fresh to-day as when it was written, it shows clearly that it anticipated the hectic temper that we have had in Negro literature and music since the war. At the close the character of whom we have spoken has decided, after many misgivings, to remain beyond the color-line. He is not satisfied, however. He attends a meeting in Carnegie Hall, hears Booker T. Washington speak and the Hampton students sing, and he feels that he too, had he not been small and selfish, might have made his life great, and been part of the glorious work of making a race.

In 1917 appeared Mr. Johnson's strongest collection of verse, "Fifty Years and Other Poems," which also came out some years later in a new edition and with a new publisher. The title poem in noble stanzas celebrates the anniversary of freedom, with a call to courage for the future, and there is a section of "Jingles and Croons" including the threnody "Sence You Went Away." Chief distinction, however, attaches to such pieces as had appeared in *The Century Magazine,* one of the best being that in which the poet praises the unknown makers of the Negro melodies.

O black and unknown bards of long ago,
  How came your lips to touch the sacred fire?
How, in your darkness, did you come to know
  The power and beauty of the minstrel's lyre?
Who first from 'midst his bonds lifted his eyes?
  Who first from out the still watch, lone and long,
Feeling the ancient faith of prophets rise
  Within his dark-kept soul, burst into song?

There is a wide, wide wonder in it all,
  That from degraded rest and servile toil,
The fiery spirit of the seer should call
  These simple children of the sun and soil.
O black singers, gone, forgot, unfamed,
  You—you alone, of all the long, long line
Of those who've sung untaught, unknown, unnamed,
  Have stretched out upward, seeking the divine.

You sang not deeds of heroes or of kings:
  No chant of bloody war, nor exulting pæan
Of arms-won triumphs; but your humble strings
  You touched in chords with music empyrean.
You sang far better than you knew, the songs
  That for your listeners' hungry hearts sufficed
Still live—but more than this to you belongs:
  You sang a race from wood and stone to Christ.

In 1922 Mr. Johnson brought out an anthology, "The Book of American Negro Poetry," with an Introduction that was a notable contribution to the literature of the subject. Five years later appeared "God's

Trombones: Seven Negro Sermons in Verse,'' in which the author endeavored to catch something of what is frequently the powerful imagery of the uneducated Negro preacher. The subjects, such as ''The Creation,'' ''Noah Built the Ark,'' and ''The Judgment Day,'' were singularly adapted to the purpose. About the same time also appeared ''The Book of American Negro Spirituals'' and ''The Second Book of American Negro Spirituals,'' with scholarly Introductions by James Weldon Johnson and with the music transcribed or arranged by Rosamond Johnson. The last three books mentioned were all in the mood of the hour and won widespread popularity.

Life is paradoxical, however, and Fame a capricious personage. It is not what the crowd applauds that most often has the seal of the ages. In the case of Mr. Johnson, it is not necessarily the popular books that have appeared in recent years by which he will ultimately best be known. We rather go back to the days of struggle, of aspiration and infinite yearning, to the years of ''Lift Ev'ry Voice and Sing,'' ''O Black and Unknown

Bards," and "The Young Warrior." The man who wrote these things made a permanent contribution to his country; and when we consider this author as one of the writers of the Negro race, we find that there is no one living who has done work that is more significant or that is more likely to be enduring.

X

IN addition to those who have been mentioned, there have been scores of writers who would have to be considered if we were dealing with the literature of the Negro in the widest sense of the term. Not too clearly, however, can the limitations of our subject be insisted upon. We are here concerned with distinctly literary or artistic achievement, and not with work that belongs primarily in the realm of religion, sociology, or politics. Only brief mention accordingly can be given to these other fields.

Naturally, from the first there have been works dealing with the place of the Negro in American life. Outstanding are the books of Booker T. Washington. Representative of these are "The Future of the American Negro," "My Larger Education," and "The Man Farthest Down." In the years just before the Civil War, Henry Highland Garnet

wrote sermons and addresses on the status of
the race in America; and Martin R. Delany
wrote a thoughtful little book, "The Condition, Elevation, Emigration, and Destiny of
the Colored People of the United States,
Politically Considered." After the war,
Alexander Crummell became an outstanding
figure by reason of his sermons and addresses;
and he was followed by an interesting group
of able men, represented especially by William
S. Scarborough, Kelly Miller, and Archibald
H. Grimké. Scarborough served for years as
professor or as president at Wilberforce
University, and contributed numerous articles
to representative magazines. His work in
more technical fields is represented by his
"First Lessons in Greek," a treatise on the
"Birds" of Aristophanes, and his paper in
The Arena (January, 1897) on "Negro Folk-
Lore and Dialect." Mr. Miller has given
long service as one of the deans at Howard
University, and he has collected several of
his cogent papers in two volumes, "Race
Adjustment" and "Out of the House of
Bondage." The first is the more varied and
interesting of the two books, but the second

contains the poetic rhapsody, "I See and Am Satisfied," first published in *The Independent* (August 7, 1913). Mr. Grimké, as well as Mr. Miller, has contributed to *The Atlantic Monthly;* and he has written the lives of Garrison and Sumner in the American Reformers Series.

Numerous have been the efforts in the field of biography and autobiography. In 1878 appeared James M. Trotter's "Music and Some Highly Musical People," and in 1887 "Men of Mark," by William J. Simmons. John Mercer Langston's "From the Virginia Plantation to the National Capitol" gives many sidelights on American history; special interest attaches to Matthew Henson's "A Negro Explorer at the North Pole;" and Maud Cuney Hare's "Norris Wright Cuney" was a distinct contribution to the history of Southern politics. The most widely known work in this field, however, is "Up From Slavery," by Booker T. Washington. The simple and unaffected style of this book has made it a model of personal writing, and it is by reason of merit that the work has gained unusual currency. Dr. Washington's successor at Tuskegee, Robert Russa Moton, has written "Finding a Way Out," an autobiography that in simple and charming manner throws many sidelights on life in Virginia a generation ago. More recently he has issued "What the Negro Thinks."

In 1872, full of personal experience, appeared William Still's "The Underground Railroad." The epoch-making work in history, however, was the two-volume "History of the Negro Race in America" (1883), by George W. Williams. This production was the exploration of a new field and the result of seven years of study. The historian more than once wrote subjectively, and after forty years many of his pages have naturally been superseded; at the same time the work was, on the whole, in unusually good taste, and even to-day in many chapters it will be found to be a storehouse for students of the subject. Largely original in the nature of their contribution were "The Haitian Revolution," by T. G. Steward, and "The Facts of Reconstruction," by John R. Lynch; while J. W. Cromwell's "The Negro in American History," mainly biographical, is interesting and stimulating throughout. Technical study in recent years is well represented by Dr. Carter G. Woodson's "The Education of the Negro Prior to 1861." Dr. Woodson has also written "The Negro in our History" and "A Century of Migration," and edited various volumes, prominent among these being "Negro Orators and their Orations." He is editor of *The Journal of Negro History* and director of the work of the Association for the Study of Negro Life and History. In 1926 he was awarded the Spingarn Medal. In this general connection mention might also be made of "A Short History of the American Negro" and "A Social History of the American Negro," by the author of the present volume.

In the field of poetry, all who went before him were of course surpassed by Dunbar, and this poet started a tradition. All over the country there sprang up imitators, and some of the imitations were more than fair. Independent of this influence, however, there were in the first quarter of the new century at least a score of writers whose verse would call for serious criticism. Among these were

Joseph S. Cotter, Jr., Roscoe C. Jamison, Fenton Johnson, George Reginald Margetson, and Leslie Pinckney Hill, all of whom, except the first two, are still living. All are represented in one or more of the collections, Johnson's "The Book of American Negro Poetry," Kerlin's "Negro Poets and their Poems," and White and Jackson's "Poetry by American Negroes." Cotter's "The Band of Gideon" shows the influence of Vachel Lindsay and anticipates the note of our next chapter.

> The band of Gideon roam the sky,
> The howling wind is their war-cry,
> The thunder's roll is their trumpet's peal
> And the lightning's flash their vengeful steel.
> > Each black cloud
> > Is a fiery steed;
> > And they cry aloud
> > With each strong deed,
> "The Sword of the Lord and Gideon."

Jamison's "Negro Soldiers" is representative of the nobler spirit that moved the race in the troublous days of the war.

> These truly are the Brave,
> These men who cast aside
> Old memories, to walk the blood-stained pave
> Of Sacrifice, joining the solemn tide

That moves away, to suffer and to die
For Freedom—when their own is yet denied!
O Pride! O Prejudice! When they pass by,
Hail them, the Brave, for you now crucified!

These truly are the Free,
These souls that grandly rise
Above base dreams of vengeance for their wrongs,
Who march to war with visions in their eyes
Of Peace through Brotherhood, lifting glad songs
Aforetime, while they front the firing-line.
Stand and behold! They take the field today,
Shedding their blood like Him now held divine,
That those who mock might find a better way!

Mr. Hill, for several years now head of the State Normal School at Cheyney, Penn., is the author of a collection, "The Wings of Oppression," and a long poem, "Toussaint L'Ouverture."

Among those who have made good contribution in recent years are several women. Alice Dunbar Nelson is known not only for her poetry but also for "The Goodness of St. Rocque, and Other Stories." The high standard unto which her verse sometimes attains may be seen from the sonnet "Violets:"

I had not thought of violets of late,
The wild, shy kind that spring beneath your feet
In wistful April days, when lovers mate

And wander through the fields in raptures sweet.
The thoughts of violets meant florists' shops,
And bows and pins, and perfumed papers fine;
And garish lights, and mincing little fops,
And cabarets and songs, and deadening wine.
So far from sweet real things my thoughts had
    strayed,
I had forgot wide fields and clear brown streams;
The perfect loveliness that God has made—
Wild violets shy and Heaven-mounting dreams;
And now unwittingly, you've made me dream
Of violets, and my soul's forgotten gleam.

Georgia Douglas Johnson is the author of three small volumes, "The Heart of a Woman," "Bronze," and "An Autumn Love Cycle." While the second of these is devoted to themes of interest to the Negro, the work of this author for the most part does not have special racial significance. In her earlier verse she emphasized the poignant, sharply chiselled lyric that became so popular a decade or more ago. Within the last few years, however, there has come into her work a deeper, a more mellow note, as in "I closed My Shutters Fast Last Night:"

> I closed my shutters fast last night,
> Reluctantly and slow,
> So pleading was the purple sky

With all the lights hung low;
I left my lagging heart outside
Within the dark alone,
I heard it singing through the gloom
A wordless, anguished tone.

Upon my sleepless couch I lay
Until the tranquil morn
Came through the silver silences
To bring my heart forlorn,
Restoring it with calm caress
Unto its sheltered bower,
While whispering: "Await, await
Your golden, perfect hour."

Jessie Fauset, who is later to be mentioned
in connection with the novel, is also the author
of some good poems, "Christmas Eve in
France" having appeared first in *The Independent*. Anne Spencer has chosen free
verse as the medium for her distinctive work.
Angelina W. Grimké, author of "Rachel," a
play in three acts, has written lyrics that are
often vivid and highly suggestive. The clear-
cut quality of her work may be seen in the
four lines entitled "Dusk:"

Twin stars through my purpling pane,
  The shriveling husk
Of a yellowing moon on the wane—
  And the dusk.

XI

ONE day toward the close of the war a man from Jamaica, Marcus Garvey, rode through the streets of New York in gay apparel as president of the Provisional Republic of Africa, head of the Universal Negro Improvement Association and African Communities League of the World, and president of the Black Star Line of steamships and the Negro Factories Corporation. The central thought that appealed to hosts of people and won their support was that of freedom for the race in every sense of the word. Such freedom, it was maintained, transcended the mere demand for political and social rights, and could only be realized under a vast supergovernment controlling the destiny of the race in Africa and throughout the world. It was asserted that the time had come for the Negro to cease depending upon favors grudg-

ingly wrested from white men and to rely
solely on his own resources and the might of
his own right arm. Conservative men of the
race held aloof from Mr. Garvey's grandiose
schemes, and after a while his career went
into eclipse; nevertheless, as no other man
of the race, he had given to the soul of the
Negro a new sense of freedom. His influence
on the literature that we are now to consider
was inestimable.

That literature, like most produced in
America in recent years, has been realistic,
and to some extent analytic. The increased
racial self-respect was a very solid gain; but
there were also some liabilities. The new
order of things brought into prominence that
quality in the Negro—romanticism—which
was at once his greatest gift and his greatest
pitfall. In some quarters, with his love of
song and the dance, he gave himself to the
most intense living. For the moment, however, all America was abnormal; old modes
of thought and conduct were in the crucible;
and the popular demand for the exotic and the
exciting was met by a strident form of music
originating in Negro slums and known as

jazz. Along with this was a mood that was of the very essence of hedonism and paganism. Introspection and self-pity ran riot; psycho-analysis became the accepted mode; and the result was a new form of so-called art known as the "blues," the spirit of which may be seen from the following:

Everybody in Hoboken town—everybody an' me
Hopped upon a warehouse that was swinging
    around
An' went to sea;
Oh, all day long I's looking for trees—
Lookin' for sand, lookin' for land,
'Cause I've got dose awful, weepin', sleepin',
Got dose awful sailin', wailin',
Got dose awful deep sea blues.

Such influences as have been described received strong re-enforcement from the band conducted by James Reese Europe in the course of the war. This organization was connected with the 369th United States Infantry Regiment (the old 15th New York); it made a specialty of jazz music; and about the close of the war it was exceedingly popular with the American Expeditionary Forces and throughout France.

On its more serious side the new temper

was admirably represented by such a collection as "The New Negro," edited by Alain Locke, or "Ebony and Topaz," edited by Charles S. Johnson. In a more general way there were three results in literature and art. The first was a lack of regard for any accepted standards whatsoever. Young writers were led to believe that they did not need any training in technique, and the popular form of poetizing known as "free verse" was most acceptable because most unrestrained. In prose the desired outlet was found in a sharp staccato form of writing that a few popular authors of the day had used as a medium but that attacked the very foundations of grammar. The second result of the dominant mood was a preference for sordid, unpleasant, or forbidden themes. The third was a certain blatant quality, an obvious striving for effect, that frequently gave an impression of artificiality.

Three men—Eric Walrond, Claude McKay, and Countee Cullen—are outstanding in the new school; but, paradoxical as it may seem, no one of the three fully represents the tendencies that have been remarked, each having

some definite vision as an artist. In some
ways they may be representative; but it has
remained for some others not quite so strong,
the imitators, to give free rein to their steeds
and to go to the extreme. With the whole
group, however, that part of New York
known as Harlem has been an obsession.
Because this section was close to the publishers' houses, and because most of the
Negroes in the metropolis lived there, the
tendency has been to regard it as in a literary
way the center of the Negro world. It is
obvious that the literature of the race can
not be free, can not be genuinely creative,
until this burden is shaken off, and that for
the true study of Negro life we must still go
to the South, where most of the men and
women live and labor. The musicians know
this; the novelists must learn it also.

Mr. Walrond was born in British Guiana
in 1898 and in his youth gained wide acquaintance with the West Indies. He came
to New York in 1918, studied at the College
of the City of New York and at Columbia,
and a little later was on the staff of *Opportunity*. In 1926 he brought forth "Tropic

Death," a work showing genuine and independent power. The book is a collection of ten stories or sketches that deal with the tragedy in the lives of the poorer people in the West Indies. Sometimes death comes to the Negro peasant through drought or starvation, sometimes through lingering and loathsome disease; or it may be that a drunken marine pulls a trigger to uphold the established order. The book is not always a pleasant one, nor is it a perfect one. Some of the stories are episodic, and frequently the suggestion is so veiled that even the diligent reader is puzzled. "Drought" and "Subjection," however, leave no doubt as to the author's ability. A later work is "The Big Ditch," a study of the human elements centered about the Panama Canal. In general Mr. Walrond excels other writers in the freshness of his material, in his clear perception of what has value, and in the strength of his style. It would seem that there is little in the art of fiction that is beyond his capabilities.

Mr. McKay is also from abroad. Born in Jamaica in 1889, he came to the United States in 1912, studied for two years at the Kansas State University, was for a while associate editor of *The Liberator* and *The Masses,* and has since spent considerable time in Russia, Germany, and France. He first attracted attention with a daring sonnet, "Harlem Dancer;" and in the course of the war the lines "If We Must Die" were much quoted. The intensity and force, if not the poignancy, of much of his work, are represented by the sonnet "White Houses:"

Your door is shut against my tightened face,
And I am sharp as steel with discontent;
But I possess the courage and the grace
To bear my anger proudly and unbent.
The pavement slabs burn loose beneath my feet,
A chafing savage, down the decent street;
And passion rends my vitals as I pass,
Where boldly shines your shuttered door of glass.
Oh, I must search for wisdom every hour,
Deep in my wrathful bosom sore and raw,
And find in it the superhuman power
To hold me to the letter of your law!
Oh, I must keep my heart inviolate
Against the potent poison of your hate.

Something of this writer's quality may also be seen in "Flame-Heart," a poem of superb power.

I still recall the honey-fever grass,
  But can not recollect the high days when
We rooted them out of the ping-wing path
  To stop the mad bees in the rabbit pen.
I often try to think in what sweet mouth
  The languid painted ladies used to dapple
The yellow by-road mazing from the main,
  Sweet with the golden-threads of the rose-apple.
I have forgotten—strange—but quite remember
The poinsettia's red, blood-red in warm December.

In 1922 Mr. McKay brought together the
best of his verse in "Harlem Shadows;" and
six years later he published a novel, "Home
to Harlem," giving a vivid portrayal of lower
class life in New York and Philadelphia, and
then "Banjo," in similar vein but with setting in Europe. One can not always applaud
his selection of subjects; nevertheless he has
firm command of his material and generally
secures the effect he sets out to achieve.

Mr. Cullen, born in New York in 1903,
wrote verses in his youth, took degrees at
New York University and Harvard, and for
a while served as associate editor of *Opportunity*. He has contributed to outstanding
magazines and taken several valuable prizes.
His first collection, "Color," appeared in

1925; his second, "Copper Sun," in 1927; in this same year also an anthology, "Caroling Dusk." This last production included the work of most of the older writers but is distinctly modern in tone and makes a feature of the work of younger singers. From Dunbar eight poems are taken, but none are in dialect. In the work of James Weldon Johnson "O Black and Unknown Bards" and the sonnet "Mother Night" are passed over for "The Creation" and "The White Witch." Among the younger writers whose work is given place are Helene Johnson, Blanche Taylor Dickinson, Arna Bontemps, Frank Horne, Sterling A. Brown, Waring Cuney, and George Leonard Allen. Mr. Cullen's own work has so far shown a tendency unduly to crowd lines with consonant effects, but that he has the spirit of a genuine poet may be seen from the following eight lines from "Ballad of the Brown Girl:"

> O lovers, never barter love
>   For gold or fertile lands,
> For love is meat and love is drink,
>   And love heeds love's commands.

And love is shelter from the rain,
    And scowling stormy skies;
Who casts off love must break his heart,
    And rue it till he dies.

Three other men call for mention in this
connection—Jean Toomer, Langston Hughes,
and Rudolph Fisher. Toomer in 1923 published a poetic novel, "Cane," that in some
portions indicated distinct power. The representative volume of Hughes is "The Weary
Blues" (1926), in the manner of Vachel Lindsay's "The Congo." Fisher has written
some strong short stories; "The City of
Refuge" appeared in the *Atlantic*.

Quite distinct from the school that we have
been considering, but still realistic in method,
is another group of writers, one mainly devoted to treating in the guise of fiction different problems in the life of the Negro. In
the main Jessie Fauset, author of "There is
Confusion" and "Plum Bun," and Nella
Larsen (Mrs. Imes), author of "Quicksand"
and "Passing," have been concerned with
the lot of the woman of unusual attractive-
ness face to face with the ways of the world.
In "Plum Bun" Angela Murray goes forth

to market to buy a plum bun only to come
back at last disillusioned. "Passing" shows
an excellent sense of form and is an especially promising performance. It is the
story of Clare Kendry, white "with a touch
of the tar-brush," who marries away from
her people only to be brought back to
them by a yearning that ends in tragedy.
The best known writer in this group, however, is Walter F. White, who was educated
at Atlanta University and who has served for
some years as Assistant Executive Secretary
of the National Association for the Advancement of Colored People. In his work the
propaganda is deliberate, though one may
well ask why a writer should not use propaganda if he wants his work to have vitality.
In "The Fire in the Flint" (1925) there is
an abundance of philosophizing, and the
workmanship, especially near the beginning,
is uncertain; but, before the book gets
through, it presents a situation that grips the
reader with its power and that sweeps all
before it to a harrowing but inevitable close.
"Flight" (1926) was on the whole not so
successful; the first part of the book is not

firmly organized and the latter portion was evidently hastily done. The work, however, attempts something a little finer than "The Fire in the Flint;" and the flight of the heroine and her struggle back to respectability hold the interest firmly. "Rope and Faggot" (1929), "a Biography of Judge Lynch," presents graphically the result of ten years of investigation of America's most disgraceful institution.

XII

IN no other field has the Negro with artistic aspirations found the road so hard as in that of the classic drama. In spite of the far-reaching influence of the Negro on American life, it is only within very recent years that this distinct racial element has received serious attention in the theater. Shakespeare's Othello was professedly a Moor rather than a Negro, and the play to which he gave his name is the supreme achievement in English in dramatic technique; nevertheless he has been a constant source of embarrassment in the western world, and on the American stage his color has often been so lightened that one could only guess at his racial connections. When in 1696 Thomas Southerne adapted "Oroonoko" from the novel of Mrs. Aphra Behn and presented in London the story of the African prince fallen on evil days, still no one saw any reason why the Negro should not be a subject for tragedy. In 1768, however, was presented at Drury Lane a comic opera, *The Padlock,* and a prominent character was Mungo, the slave of a West Indian planter, who got drunk in the second act and was profane throughout the performance. The depreciation of the race thus started continued, and when in 1781 "Robinson Crusoe" was given as a panto-mime in Drury Lane, Friday was represented as a Negro. The development of Negro min-strelsy in the course of the next century, and the antics of Topsy in "Uncle Tom's Cabin," only accelerated a movement that had already begun.

That the Negro could succeed on the legiti-mate stage, however, was shown by such a career as that of Ira Aldridge. This dis-tinguished actor, making his way from Mary-land to the freer life of Europe, entered upon the period of his greatest success when, in 1833, at Covent Garden, he played Othello to the Iago of Kean, the foremost actor of the time. He was universally ranked as a great tragedian. In the years 1852-5 he played in

Germany. In 1857 the King of Sweden invited him to visit Stockholm. The King of Prussia bestowed upon him a first class medal of the arts and sciences. The Emperor of Austria gave him an autograph letter; and the Czar of Russia bestowed upon him a decoration.

Such is the noblest tradition of the Negro on the stage. Aside from "Uncle Tom's Cabin" moreover, there was effort at serious portrayal in "The Octoroon" (1859), by Dion Boucicault. In course of time, however, because of the popularity of blackface minstrelsy, all association of the Negro with the classic drama was effectively erased from the public mind. Near the turn of the century some outlet was found in light musical comedy. Prominent in the transition from minstrelsy to the new form was Ernest Hogan; and representative companies were those of Cole and Johnson, and Williams and Walker. Bert (Egbert Austin) Williams became one of the foremost comedians on the American stage and a member of "The Follies;" and plans for higher things were being made for him when he died in 1922.

About the time of his passing, and later, such shows as ''Shuffle Along,'' ''Runnin' Wild,'' and ''Blackbirds'' were popular; and these brought prominently before the public another star, Florence Mills, who with a remarkable personality lifted light entertainment to the plane of art. When she died in the autumn of 1927 the New York Times said: ''Her fame in the international theater is more than a sign of the advancement of Negroes. She was one of the leaders whose accomplishment sets the whole racial movement a notch or two forward. No special plea for lenient judgment was suggested in her work. None was needed. The quality of her performance, the very timbre of her voice, cut the ground from under the critic who might have liked to patronize. [She did her work] with an air of childlike enjoyment, knowing how good it was, certain of delighting her audience, performing always with a relish and assurance as far removed as possible from conceit.''

Meanwhile, from time to time, there was experiment in the legitimate drama, either with Negro actors or with plays using Negro themes. In the spring of 1914 a one-act play,

"Granny Maumee," by Ridgely Torrence, was produced by the Stage Society of New York, the part of the central figure being taken by Dorothy Donnelly, one of the most sincere of American actresses. In April, 1917, "Granny Maumee," with two other one-act plays by Mr. Torrence, "The Rider of Dreams" and "Simon the Cyrenian," was again put on the stage in New York, this time with a company of Negro actors, the production being advertised as "the first colored dramatic company to appear on Broadway." In the spring of 1916 the Edward Sterling Wright Players made a favorable impression in the legitimate drama, especially in "Othello;" and about the same time the Lafayette Players in New York made commendable progress in the production of popular plays.

Then suddenly the serious play of Negro life broke through to public favor and critical approval. It was in the 90's that Charles S. Gilpin began his career as a variety performer in Richmond, Va. In 1903 he was one of the Gilmore Canadian Jubilee Singers; in 1905 he was with Williams and Walker; the

CHARLES S. GILPIN AS "THE EMPEROR JONES"

next season with Gus Hill's "Smart Set;" and then, from 1907 to 1909, with the Pekin Stock Company of Chicago. This last company consisted of about forty members, of whom eleven were finally selected for serious drama. Mr. Gilpin was one of these; but the manager died, and once more the aspiring actor was forced back to vaudeville.

Now followed ten long years—years of the kind that blast and kill, and with which the strongest man sometimes goes under. With the managers in New York there was no opening; and yet there was hope—not only hope but leadership and effort for others, as when Mr. Gilpin carried a company of his own to the Lafayette Theater, beginning the production of the popular plays of which we have spoken. Life was leading—somewhere; but meanwhile one had to live, and the way was very uncertain. At last, in 1919, came a chance to play William Custis, the old Negro in Drinkwater's "Abraham Lincoln." The part was not a great one, but it led to engagement as the star of "The Emperor Jones," by Eugene O'Neill, in the autumn of 1920; and Mr. Gilpin's work in this part was one

of the features of the New York theatrical
season of 1920-21. At the annual dinner of
the Drama League in 1921 he was one of the
ten guests who were honored as having contributed most to the American theater during
the year; just a few months later he was
awarded the Spingarn Medal.

The play on which this success was based
is a highly dramatic study of panic and fear.
The Emperor Jones is a Negro who has
broken out of jail in the United States and
escaped to what is termed "a West Indian
island not yet self-determined by white
marines." Here he is sufficiently bold and
ingenious to make himself ruler within two
years. He moves unharmed among his sullen
subjects by virtue of a legend of his invention
that only a silver bullet can harm him; but at
length, when he has reaped all the riches in
sight, he deems it advisable to flee. As the
play begins, the measured sound of a beating
tom-tom in the hills gives warning that the
natives are in conclave, using all kinds of
incantations to work themselves up to the
point of rebellion. Nightfall finds the Emperor at the edge of a forest where he has

food hidden and through whose trackless waste he knows a way to safety and freedom. His revolver carries five bullets for his pursuers and a silver one for himself in case of need. Bold and adventurous, he plunges into the jungle at sunset; but at dawn, half-crazed, naked, and broken, he stumbles back to the starting-place, only to find the natives quietly waiting for him. Now follows a vivid succession of strange sounds and shadows, with terrible visions from the past. As the Emperor's fear quickens, the forest seems filled with threatening people who stare at and bid for him. Finally, shrieking at the worst vision of all, he is driven back to the clearing and to his death, the tom-tom beating ever faster as the fatal moment nears.

To the demands of this remarkable part—so dominating that it has been called a dramatic monologue—Mr. Gilpin brought the resources of a matured and thoroughly capable actor; and for once the critics were agreed in their verdict. Since 1921 the part has also been played by Paul Robeson, a man gifted as singer as well as actor, who has taken the leading rôle in another one of O'Neill's plays,

"All God's Chillun Got Wings." Evelyn Preer and Rose McClendon are also among those who in special parts have won critical approval by their earnest and intelligent effort.

Joseph W. Krutch, writing in *The Nation* (October 26, 1927), has given a criticism that is well worth the attention of all who are interested in the advance of the Negro in the legitimate drama. Says he: "Those who have watched the Negro actor on Broadway must often have observed how fundamentally the character of his art differs from that of his white fellows. . . . Ecstasy seems to be his natural state. While our own actors pant after an emotion and must depend for their outburst upon elaborately learned tricks, he, on the contrary, is good only when some utter abandonment is to be portrayed. He may move awkwardly, almost uncomprehendingly, through level scenes which the most mediocre of general utility men could carry off with competence, but he leaps with an effortless joy into a crisis and surrenders himself to joy, to terror, or to grief, as to a native element. And, above all, he catches the con-

tagion of a group. His voice swells with the
swelling of other voices; his body catches the
rhythm of a crowd; and he reveals an in-
stinctive sense for participation in an emotion larger than his comprehension. One
searches for a word to describe his abandonment and one discovers that the word is
Dionysian—that his gift is a gift for drama
in a form more primitive as well as, perhaps,
more purely dramatic than that of our conventional stage, which is no more than a
platform where the decorous conversations
of decorous life are recited. . . . The dra-
matization of the novel 'Porgy' is one which
affords a great many opportunities for just
such casting. Most of the action takes place
either in the courtyard of a swarming
Charleston tenement or in the room of one
of its denizens where the community gathers
to hold a wake; and the effects are created
by a succession of mass scenes in the course
of which the performers succeed in convey-
ing to the spectator a sense of life in a community which, for all its ignorance and
squalor, lives passionately and as a unit. The
whole is, indeed, a highly interesting and, in

part, very successful attempt to translate a novel into purely theatrical terms; and if the method were carried only a little further it would result in a type of play in which ordinary dialogue had been completely replaced by the pageant, the pantomime, and the chant of the ritualistic drama.''

In general it is obvious that while within recent years the Negro has made only a beginning, he has at least made a very real beginning in the legitimate drama. Such success as that of Mr. Gilpin was of the highest significance. Meanwhile at the representative Negro colleges plays by standard dramatists have been given frequent production. All such work is very valuable as giving to young performers fundamental training in appreciation and technique; but it must not be forgotten that if the Negro is to make a genuine contribution to the dream in America, he must mainly look into his own life and depend on his own resources. Just as Shakespeare revealed the age of Elizabeth in his mighty line, so must the Negro dramatist, if he would be successful, set forth the life of his own people with all their humors and strivings. Any effort with this end in view is in the right direction and, if earnest, should be given all possible encouragement.

XIII

PAINTING has long been a medium through which the spirit of the race yearned to find expression. As far back as in the work of Phillis Wheatley there is a poem addressed to "S. M." (Scipio Moorehead), "a young African Painter," one of whose subjects was the story of Damon and Pythias. It was a hundred years more, however, before there was genuinely artistic production. E. M. Bannister, whose home was in Providence, though little known to the younger generation, was very prominent fifty years ago. He gathered about him a coterie of artists and men of means who formed the nucleus of the Rhode Island Art Club, and one of his pictures took a medal at the Centennial Exposition of 1876. William A. Harper, who died in 1910, was a product of the Chicago Art Institute, at whose exhibi-

138

HENRY O. TANNER

tions his pictures received much favorable comment. After he had spent a season of study in Paris, his "Avenue of Poplars" took a prize of one hundred dollars at the Institute. Other subjects were "The Last Gleam," "The Hillside," and "The Gray Dawn." Great hopes were awakened a few years ago by the landscapes of Richard L. Brown; and several years ago the portrait work of Edwin A. Harleston began to attract the attention of the discerning.

William E. Scott, of Indianapolis, is becoming more and more distinguished in mural work, landscape, and portraiture, and among all the painters of the race now working in this country is outstanding. After some years at the Art Institute in Chicago, where he had to work very hard but where he also took numerous prizes, he journeyed to Paris to continue his studies. Here there were difficulties innumerable to be met; but he made progress in various academies, worked for a while in the studio of Tanner, and at last, in 1912, saw one of his paintings, "La Pauvre Voisine," accepted at the autumn Salon. For this achievement he received great praise in the French newspapers, and the Argentine Government, having heard about the picture, bought it for six hundred dollars. A second picture, "La Misère," exhibited in 1913, was reproduced in the French catalogue, and the next year took first prize at the Indiana State Fair. In 1913 also "La Connoisseure" was exhibited at the Royal Academy in London. In 1918 the city of Indianapolis paid a tribute to a native son by purchasing "A Rainy Night in Etaples." Mr. Scott in recent years has given his attention more and more to mural work. For a bank in Edwardsville, Illinois, he executed a commission for a painting illustrating the signing of the treaty between the Indians and Governor Edwards in 1819. Other mural paintings include those for the City Hospital, Indianapolis, the State House at Springfield, Illinois, the Court House at Fort Wayne, Indiana, a large Catholic church in Chicago, the First Presbyterian Church of Chicago, and many for public schools throughout the country. The commission from the city of Indianapolis called for work on not less than three hundred life-size figures. In several other pictures Mr. Scott has emphasized racial subjects.

Within the last few years several other persons have attracted favorable attention by their paintings or drawings, and have been encouraged by Harmon awards or special prizes. Prominent among these are Laura Wheeler Waring, Palmer C. Hayden, Hale Woodruff, Archibald J. Motley, Jr., Malvin Gray Johnson, and Aaron Douglas. Three of Mr. Motley's subjects are "Octoroon Girl," "The Picnic at the Grove," and "Mending Socks." He also excels in the portrayal of African jungle life. Mr. Douglas is more modern in tone than most of the others and has had drawings in "The New Negro" and numerous other publications. All of these artists, however, are just at the beginning of their careers, and only time can tell to what extent they will be able to realize their dreams.

The painter of assured fame and commanding position is Henry Ossawa Tanner. The early years of this artist were years of singular struggle and sacrifice. At the age of thirteen, seeing an artist at work, he decided that he too would be a painter, and he later entered the Pennsylvania Academy of Fine Arts. While still a very young man, he attempted drawings of all sorts and sent these to various New York publishers, only to see them returned. A check for forty dollars, however, for one that did not return encouraged him, and a picture, "A Lion at Home," from the exhibition of the Academy of Design, brought eighty dollars. He now became a photographer in Atlanta, Ga., but met with no real success; and for two years he taught drawing at Clark University. In this period came a summer of struggle in the mountains of North Carolina, and the knowledge that a picture that had originally sold for fifteen dollars had brought two hundred and fifty at an auction in Philadelphia. Desiring now to go to Europe, the young painter gave in Cincinnati an exhibition of his work. The exhibition failed; not a picture was regularly sold. Bishop and Mrs. Hartzell, however, gave the artist a sum for the entire collection, and, thus equipped, he sailed for

Rome January 4, 1891, going by way of Liverpool and Paris.

In the story of his career that he contributed to *The World's Work* some years ago, Mr. Tanner gave an interesting account of his early days in Paris. Acquaintance with the French capital induced him to abandon all thought of going to Rome; but there followed five years of pitiless economy, broken only by a visit to Philadelphia, where he sold some pictures. He was encouraged, however, by Benjamin Constant, and studied in the Julien Academy. In his early years he had given attention to animals and landscape, but more and more he was drawn toward religious subjects. "Daniel in the Lions' Den" in the Salon of 1896 brought "honorable mention," the artist's first official recognition. He was inspired, and soon afterwards he made his first visit to Palestine, the land that was later to mean so much to him in his work. "The Resurrection of Lazarus" (1897) was bought by the French Government and now hangs in the Luxembourg. The enthusiasm awakened by this production was so great that a friend wrote to the painter at Venice: "Come home, Tanner, to see the crowds behold your picture." After twenty years of heart-breaking effort Henry O. Tanner had become a recognized artist. His later career is a part of the history of the world's art. He won medals at the Salon in 1897 and 1907, at the Paris Exposition in 1900, at the Buffalo Exposition in 1901, at St. Louis in 1904, at San Francisco in 1915, the Walter Lippincott Prize in Philadelphia in 1900, and, in 1906, the Harris Prize of five hundred dollars for the best picture in the annual exhibition of American paintings at the Chicago Art Institute.

"The Annunciation" now hangs in Memorial Hall in Fairmount Park in Philadelphia. "Christ and Nicodemus" was purchased by the Pennsylvania Academy of Fine Arts. "The Bagpipe Lesson" and "The Banjo Lesson" are in the Library at Hampton Institute. Other representative titles are "Moses and the Burning Bush," "Jews Waiting at the Wall of Solomon," "A Flight Into Egypt," "Christ and His Disciples on the Road to Bethany," "Stephen before the Council," "The Mothers of the

The Banjo Lesson

BY HENRY O. TANNER

Bible" (a series of five paintings of Mary, Hagar, Sarah, Rachel, and the mother of Moses, that marked the commencement of paintings containing all or nearly all female pictures), "Christ at the Home of Mary and Martha," "The Five Virgins," and "The Return of the Holy Women." Of "A Flight into Egypt" the artist said: "Never shall I forget the magnificence of two Persian Jews that I once saw at Rachel's Tomb; what a magnificent 'Abraham' either one of them would have made! Nor do I forget a ride one stormy Christmas night to Bethlehem. Dark clouds swept the moonlit skies, and it took little imagination to close one's eyes to the flight of time and see in those hurrying travelers the crowds that hurried toward Bethlehem on that memorable night of the Nativity, or to transpose the scene and see in each hurrying group a 'Flight into Egypt.'" As to which one of all these pictures excels the others is a question that might give critics long discussion. "The Resurrection of Lazarus" is in subdued coloring, while "The Annunciation" is distinguished by its effects of light and shade.

This latter picture must in any case rank high in a consideration of the painter's work. It is a powerful portrayal of the Virgin at the moment when she learns of her great mission.

Mr. Tanner's later life has been spent in Paris, with trips to the Far East, to Palestine, and the northern part of Africa. Some years ago he joined the colony of artists at Trepied, where he has built a commodious home and studio. Miss MacChesney has described this for us: "His studio is an ideal workroom, being high-ceilinged, spacious, and having the least possible furniture, utterly free from masses of useless studio stuff and paraphernalia. The walls are of a light gray, and at one end hangs a fine tapestry. Oriental carved wooden screens are at the doors and windows. Leading out of it is a small room having a domed ceiling and picturesque high windows. In this simply furnished room he often poses his models, painting himself in the large studio, the sliding door between being a small one. He can often make use of lamplight effects, the daylight in the larger room not interfering."

Within recent years the artist has kept pace with some of the newer schools by brilliant experimentation in color and composition. Moonlight scenes appeal to him most. He seldom paints other than biblical subjects, except perhaps a portrait such as one of the Khedive or of Rabbi Wise. A landscape may attract him, but it is sure to be idealized. He is thoroughly romantic in tone, and in spirit, if not in technique, there is much to connect him with the Pre-Raphaelite painter, Holman Hunt.

He has the highest ideals. Said he: "It has very often seemed to me that many painters of religious subjects forget that their pictures should be as much works of art as are other paintings with less holy subjects. To suppose that the fact of the religious painter having a more elevated subject than his brother artist makes it unnecessary for him to consider his picture as an artistic production, or that he can be less thoughtful about a color harmony, for instance, than he who selects any other subject, simply proves that he is less of an artist than he who gives the subject his best attention." Certainly no one could ever accuse Henry O. Tanner of insincere workmanship. His whole career is a challenge and an inspiration to aspiring painters, and his work a monument of sturdy endeavor and exalted achievement.

XIV

SCULPTORS.—META WARRICK FULLER

IN sculpture, as well as in painting, there has been a beginning of highly artistic achievement. The first person to come into prominence was Edmonia Lewis, born in New York in 1845. A sight of the statue of Franklin, in Boston, inspired within this young woman the desire also to "make a stone man." Garrison introduced her to a sculptor who encouraged her and gave her a few suggestions, but altogether she received little instruction in her art. In 1865 she attracted considerable attention by a bust of Robert Gould Shaw, exhibited in Boston. In this same year she went to Rome to continue her studies, and two years later took up her permanent residence there. Among her works are: "The Freedwoman," "The Death of Cleopatra" (exhibited at the exposition in Philadelphia in 1876), "Asleep," "The Marriage of Hiawatha," and

"Madonna with the Infant Christ." Among
her busts in terra cotta were those of John
Brown, Charles Sumner, Lincoln, and Longfellow. Most of the work of Edmonia Lewis
is in Europe. In more recent years the work of
Mrs. May Howard Jackson, of Washington,
has in increasing measure attracted the attention of the discerning. "Mother and Child" is
one of this sculptor's best studies; and she has
made several busts, among her subjects being
Rev. F. J. Grimké, Dean Kelly Miller, and
Dr. W. E. B. DuBois. She has been represented in several notable exhibitions and has
also been the recipient of a Harmon award.

The sculptor at the present time of assured position is Meta Vaux Warrick
Fuller.

Meta Vaux Warrick was born in Philadelphia, June 9, 1877. She first compelled serious recognition of her talent by her work in
the Pennsylvania School of Industrial Art,
for which she had won a scholarship, and
which she attended for four years. Here one
of her first original pieces in clay was a head
of Medusa, which, with its hanging jaw, beads
of gore, and eyes starting from their sockets,
marked her as a sculptor of the horrible. In

META WARRICK FULLER

her graduating year, 1898, she won a prize
for metal work by a crucifix upon which hung
the figure of Christ torn by anguish, also honorable mention for her work in modeling. In
her post-graduate year she won the George K.
Crozier first prize for the best general work in
modeling for the year, her particular piece
being the "Procession of Arts and Crafts."
In 1899 the young student went to Paris, where
she worked and studied for three years, chiefly
at Colarossi's Academy. Her work brought
her in contact with St. Gaudens and other
artists; and finally there came a day when
the great Rodin himself, thrilled by the figure
in "Secret Sorrow," a man represented as eating his heart out, in the attitude of a father
beamed upon the young woman and said,
"Mademoiselle, you are a sculptor; you have
the sense of form." "The Wretched," one of
the artist's masterpieces, was exhibited in the
Salon in 1903, and along with it went "The
Impenitent Thief"; and at one of Byng's exhibitions in L'Art Nouveau galleries it was remarked of her that "under her strong and
supple hands the clay has leaped into form:
a whole turbulent world seems to have forced

itself into the cold and dead material." On her return to America the artist resumed her studies at the School of Industrial Art, winning, in 1904, the Battles first prize for pottery. In 1907 she was called on for a series of tableaux representing the advance of the Negro, for the Jamestown Tercentennial Exposition, and later (1913) for a group for the New York State Emancipation Proclamation Commission. In 1909 Meta Vaux Warrick became the wife of Dr. Solomon C. Fuller, of Framingham, Mass. A disastrous fire in 1910 destroyed some of her most valuable pieces while they were in storage in Philadelphia. Only a few examples of her early work, that for one reason or another happened to be elsewhere, were saved. In May, 1914, however, she had sufficiently recovered from this blow to be able to hold a public exhibition of her work. Mrs. Fuller resides in Framingham, has a happy family of three boys, and in the midst of a busy life still finds some time for the practice of her art.

The fire of 1910 destroyed the following productions: Secret Sorrow, Silenus, Œdipus, Brittany Peasant, Primitive Man, two of the heads from Three Gray Women, Peeping Tom,

Falstaff, Oriental Dancer, Portrait of William Thomas, The Wrestlers, Death in the Wind, Désespoir, The Man with a Thorn, The Man who Laughed, the Two-Step, Sketch for a Monument, Wild Fire, and the following studies in Afro-American types: An Old Woman, The Schoolboy, The Comedian (George W. Walker), The Student, The Artist, and Mulatto Child, as well as a few unfinished pieces. Such a misfortune has only rarely befallen a rising artist. Some of the sculptor's most remarkable work was included in the list just given.

Fortunately surviving were the following: The Wretched (cast in bronze and remaining in Europe), Man Carrying Dead Body, Medusa, Procession of Arts and Crafts, Portrait of the late William Still, John the Baptist (the only piece of her work made in Paris that the sculptor now has), Sylvia (later destroyed by accident), and Study of Expression.

The exhibition of 1914 included the following: A Classic Dancer, Brittany Peasant (a reproduction of the piece destroyed), Study of Woman's Head, "A Drink, Please" (a statuette of Tommy Fuller), Mother and Baby,

A Young Equestrian (Tommy Fuller), "So Big" (Solomon Fuller, Jr.), Menelik II of Abyssinia, A Girl's Head, Portrait of a Child, The Pianist (portrait of Mrs. Maud Cuney Hare), Portrait of S. Coleridge-Taylor, Relief Study of a Woman's Head, Medallion Portrait of a Child (Tommy Fuller), Medallion Portrait of Dr. A. E. P. Rockwell, Statuette of a Woman, Second model of group made for the New York State Emancipation Proclamation Commission (with two fragments from the final model of this), Portrait of Dr. A. E. P. Rockwell, Four Figures (Spring, Summer, Autumn, Winter) for over-mantel panel, Portrait-Bust of a Child (Solomon Fuller, Jr.), Portrait-Bust of a Man (Dr. S. C. Fuller), John the Baptist, Danse Macabre, Menelik II in profile, Portrait of a Woman, The Jester.

Since 1914 the artist has produced several of her strongest pieces. "Peace Halting the Ruthlessness of War" in May, 1917, took a second prize in a competition under the auspices of the Massachusetts Branch of the Woman's Peace Party. Similarly powerful are "Watching for Dawn," "Mother and Child," "Immigrant in America," and "The Silent

Appeal." Noteworthy, too, are "The Flower-Holder," "The Fountain-Boy," and "Life in Quest of Peace." The sculptor has also produced numerous statuettes, novelties, etc., for commercial purposes, and just now she is at work on a motherhood series.

From time to time one observes in this enumeration happy subjects. Such, for instance, are "The Dancing Girl," "The Wrestlers," and "A Young Equestrian." These are frequently winsome, but, as will be shown in a moment, they are not the artist's characteristic productions. Nor was the Jamestown series of tableaux. This was a succession of fourteen groups (originally intended for seventeen) containing in all one hundred and fifty figures. The purpose was by the construction of appropriate models, dramatic groupings, and the use of proper scenic accessories, to trace in chronological order the general progress of the Negro race. The whole, of course, had its peculiar interest for the occasion; but the artist had to work against unnumbered handicaps of every sort; her work, in fact, was not so much that of a sculptor as a designer; and, while the whole production took considerable energy, she has naturally never regarded it as her representative work.

Certain productions, however, by reason of their unmistakable show of genius, call for special consideration. These are invariably tragic or serious in tone.

Prime in order, and many would say in power, is "The Wretched." Seven figures representing as many forms of human anguish greet the eye. A mother yearns for the loved ones she has lost. An old man, wasted by hunger and disease, waits for death. Another, bowed by shame, hides his face from the sun. A sick child is suffering from some terrible hereditary trouble; a youth realizes with despair that the task before him is too great for his strength; and a woman is afflicted with some mental disease. Crowning all is the philosopher, who, suffering through sympathy with the others, realizes his powerlessness to relieve them and gradually sinks into the stoniness of despair.

"The Impenitent Thief," admitted to the Salon along with "The Wretched," was demolished in 1904, after being subjected to a series of unhappy accidents. It also defied

The Wretched

BY METAWARRICK FULLER

convention. Heroic in size, the thief hung on the cross, all the while distorted by anguish. Hardened, unsympathetic, blasphemous, he was still superb in his presumption, and he was one of the artist's most powerful conceptions.

"Man Carrying Dead Body" portrays a scene from a battlefield. In it the sculptor has shown the length to which duty will spur one on. A man bears across his shoulder the body of a comrade that has evidently lain on the battlefield for days, and though the thing is horrible, he lashes it to his back and totters under the great weight until he can find a place for decent burial. To every one there comes such a duty; each one has his own burden to bear in silence.

Two earlier pieces, "Secret Sorrow," and "Œdipus," had the same marked characteristics. The first represented a man, worn and gaunt, as actually bending his head and eating out his own heart. The figure was the personification of lost ambition, shattered ideals, and despair. For "Œdipus" the sculptor chose the hero of the old Greek legend at the moment when, realizing that he has killed his father and married his mother, he tears his eyes out. The artist's later conception, "Three Gray Women," from the legend of Perseus, was in similar vein. It undertook to portray the Grææ, the three sisters who had but one eye and one tooth among them.

Perhaps the most haunting creation of Mrs. Fuller is "John the Baptist." With head slightly upraised and with eyes looking into the eternal, the prophet rises above all sordid earthly things and soars into the divine. All faith and hope and love are in his face, all poetry and inspiration in his eyes. It is a conception that, once seen, can never be forgotten.

The second model of the group for the New York State Emancipation Proclamation Commission (two feet high, the finished group as exhibited being eight feet high) represents a recently emancipated Negro youth and maiden standing beneath a gnarled, decapitated tree that has the semblance of a human hand stretched over them. Humanity is pushing them out into the world, while at the same time the hand of Fate, with obstacles and drawbacks, is restraining them in the exercise of their new freedom. In the attitudes

of the two figures is strikingly portrayed the
uncertainty of those embarking on a new life,
and in their countenances one reads all the
eagerness and the courage and the hope that
is theirs. The whole is one of the artist's
most ambitious efforts.

"Immigrant in America" was inspired by two
lines from Robert Haven Schauffler's "Scum
of the Earth":

> Children in whose frail arms shall rest
> Prophets and singers and saints of the West.

An American mother, the parent of one strong
healthy child, is seen welcoming the immigrant
mother of many children to the land of plenty.
The work is capable of wide application. Along
with it might be mentioned a suffrage medallion
and a smaller piece, "The Silent Appeal."
This last is a very strong piece of work. It
represents the mother capable of producing
and caring for three children as making a silent
request for the suffrage (or peace, or justice,
or any other noble cause). The work is char-
acterized by a singular note of dignity.

"Peace Halting the Ruthlessness of War,"
the recent prize piece, represents War as

mounted on a mighty steed and trampling to
death helpless human beings, while in one
hand he bears a spear on which he has im-
paled the head of one of his victims. As he
goes on in what seems his irresistible career
Peace meets him on the way and commands
him to cease his ravages. The work as exhibited was in gray-green wax and treated its
subject with remarkable spirit. It must take
rank as one of the four or five of the strongest productions of the artist.

More recent work includes "The Awaken-
ing of Ethiopia," which was enlarged to life
size for the Making of America Exposition
and is now in the 135th Street Branch of the
New York Public Library; and a relief portrait of Mr. Moorfield Storey, which, done in
bronze, was presented to the distinguished
publicist by the National Association for the
Advancement of Colored People on the occasion of his eightieth birthday.

Meta Warrick Fuller's work may be said
to fall into two divisions, the romantic and
the social. The first is represented by such
things as "The Wretched" and "Secret
Sorrow," the second by "Immigrant in

America'' and ''The Silent Appeal.'' The
transition may be seen in ''Watching for
Dawn,'' a group that shows seven figures, in
various attitudes of prayer, watchfulness,
and resignation, as watching for the coming
of daylight, or peace. In technique this is
like ''The Wretched,'' in spirit it is like the
later work. It is as if the sculptor's own
seer, John the Baptist, had, by his vision,
summoned her away from the ghastly and
horrible to the everyday problems of needy
humanity. There are many, however, who
hope that she will not utterly forsake the
field in which she first became famous. Her
early work is not delicate or pretty; it is
gruesome and terrible; but it is also intense
and vital, and from it speaks the very tragedy
of the Negro race.

XV

MUSIC

THE foremost name on the roll of Negro composers is that of a man whose home was in England but who in so many ways identified himself with the Negro people of the United States that he deserves to be considered here. He visited America, found the inspiration for much of his work in African themes, and his name at once comes to mind in any consideration of the Negro in music.

Samuel Coleridge-Taylor (1875-1912) was born in London, the son of a physician who was a native of Sierra Leone, and an English mother. He began the study of the violin when he was no more than six years old; at the age of ten he entered the choir of St. George's, at Croydon; and a little later he became alto singer at St. Mary Magdalene's, Croydon. In 1890 he entered the Royal College of Music as a student of the violin, and he also worked with Stanford in composition, in which department he won a scholarship in 1893. In 1894 he was graduated with honor. His earliest published work was the anthem "In Thee, O Lord" (1892); but he gave frequent performances of chamber music at student concerts in his career at the Royal College; one of his symphonies was produced in 1896 under Stanford's direction; a quintet for clarinet and strings in F sharp minor, played at the Royal College in 1895, was given in Berlin by the Joachim Quartet; and a string quartet in D minor dates from 1896. His "Ballade in A Minor," produced at the Three Choirs Festival in Gloucester in 1898, showed something of his later quality; it is distinctively Negro, and yet it never goes beyond recognized methods in harmonic, melodic, or orchestral structure. On November 11, 1898, Coleridge-Taylor became world-famous by the production at the Royal College of the first part of the "Hiawatha" trilogy, "Hiawatha's Wedding-Feast." He at once took rank as one of the foremost living English composers. The second part of the trilogy, "The Death of Minnehaha," was

given at the North Staffordshire Festival in
the autumn of 1899; and the third, "Hiawatha's Departure," by the Royal Choral
Society, in Albert Hall, March 22, 1900. The
success of the whole work was tremendous
and such as even the composer himself never
quite duplicated. Requests for new compositions for festivals now became numerous,
and in response to the demand were produced
"The Blind Girl of Castél-Cuillé" (Leeds,
1901), "Meg Blane" (Sheffield, 1902), "The
Atonement" (Hereford, 1903), and "Kubla
Khan" (Handel Society, 1906). Coleridge-
Taylor also wrote the incidental music for
the four plays by Stephen Phillips produced
at His Majesty's Theater, "Herod," Ulysses," "Nero," and "Faust;" incidental
music for "Othello" (the composition for
the orchestra being later adapted as a suite
for pianoforte) ; and that for "A Tale of Old
Japan," the words of which were by Alfred
Noyes. In 1904 he was appointed conductor
of the Handel Society. The composer's most
distinctive work is probably that reflecting
his interest in the Negro folk-song. Characteristic of the melancholy beauty, the bar-

baric color, and the passion of true Negro music are his symphonic pianoforte selections based on Negro melodies: "African Suite," "African Romances" (with words by Dunbar), "Songs of Slavery," "Three Choral Ballads," and "African Dances." The complete list of the works of Coleridge-Taylor would also include the following: "Southern Love Songs," "Dream-Lovers" (an operetta), "Gipsy Suite" (for violin and piano), "Solemn Prelude" (for orchestra, first produced at the Worcester Festival, 1899), "Nourmahal's Song and Dance" (for piano), "Scenes from an Everyday Romance," "Ethiopia Saluting the Colors" (concert march for orchestra), "Five Choral Ballads" to words by Longfellow (produced at the Norwich Festival, 1905), "Moorish Dance" (for piano), "Six Sorrow Songs," several vocal duets, and the anthems, "Now Late on the Sabbath Day," "By the Waters of Babylon," "The Lord is My Strength," "Lift Up Your Heads," "Break Forth into Joy," and "O Ye that Love the Lord." Among the things published since his death are his "Viking Song," best adapted for a male chorus, and a group of pianoforte and choral works.

In this connection, before proceeding with our consideration of what the Negro has achieved in music in the United States in recent years, it might be worth while at least to glance at a few other persons of Negro descent who have risen to distinction in other lands. George Augustus Bridgetower, violinist, born in Poland about 1779, became the friend and associate of Beethoven, with whom he played the Kreutzer Sonata at Vienna in 1805. In 1811 he received the degree of Bachelor of Music at Cambridge, and he died in England about 1845. Joseph White, born at Matanzas, Cuba, in 1836, on the advice of Gottschalk was sent to Paris in 1855. He became an honor pupil of Alard, winning in 1856 the first prize in violin playing. He composed a violin concerto and numerous smaller pieces, and in 1864 was appointed teacher in the Paris Conservatoire. In 1876 he visited the United States, playing in some of the larger cities with great success.

In this country, even before the Civil War,

there sprang up among the free Negroes of
Louisiana a number of musicians and other
artists who distinguished themselves in foreign countries where they were not held back
by prejudice. The Lambert family consisted
of seven persons, all of whom were interested in music. Richard Lambert, the father,
was a teacher; and Lucien Lambert, one of
the sons, after much hard study became a
composer. Edmund Dèdè, born in New Orleans in 1829, entered the Paris Conservatoire in 1857 and took high rank as a violinist.
He composed numerous orchestral works, the
best known being "Le Palmier Overture."
He died at Bordeaux, where for many years
he was director of the orchestra of L'Alcazar.

In the position of dean of the Negro composers in the United States to-day is Harry
T. Burleigh, who has won a place not only
among the prominent song-writers of America but of the world. His work reveals a
keen sense of melody and at the same time
great technical excellence. Among his songs
are "Jean," the "Saracen Songs," "One
Year (1914-1915)," the "Five Songs" of
Laurence Hope, and "The Young Warrior."

The popularity of this last in Italy during the war has already been remarked in connection with James W. Johnson, who wrote the words. Of somewhat stronger quality even than most of these songs are "The Grey Wolf," to words by Arthur Symons, "The Soldier," a setting of Rupert Brooke's well known sonnet, and "Ethopia Saluting the Colors." An entirely different division of Mr. Burleigh's work, hardly less important than his songs, is his various adaptations of the Negro melodies, especially for choral work, and he assisted Dvorak in his "New World Symphony," based on the Negro folksongs. For his general achievement in music he was, in 1917, awarded the Spingarn Medal. His work as a singer is reserved for later treatment.

R. Nathaniel Dett, for some years now director of music at Hampton Institute, has the merit, more than most, of attempting things in large form. While continuing his studies at Harvard in 1920-21, he won the Bowdoin essay prize with his paper "The Emancipation of Negro Music," and he also won the Francis Boott prize in composition. His

HARRY T. BURLEIGH

carol "Listen to the Lambs" is especially
worthy of note; his work for the piano is represented by his "Magnolia Suite;" and among
smaller works is his superb "Chariot Jubilee." His compositions, like the songs of
Harry T. Burleigh, are now frequently given
a place on the programs of the foremost
artists in Europe and America; and at
Hampton he has trained one of the best
choirs in the country.

Especially prominent in the day of Cole
and Johnson, and Williams and Walker in
musical comedy was Will Marion Cook.
While this composer's time has been largely
given to popular music, he has also produced
numerous songs that bear the stamp of
genius. In 1912 a group of his tuneful and
characteristic pieces was published by Schirmer. Generally his work exhibits not only
unusual melody, but also excellent technique.
J. Rosamond Johnson is also a composer with
many original ideas, and in pure melody he
is not surpassed by any other musician of the
race. Among his songs are "I Told My Love
to the Roses" and "Morning, Noon, and
Night." Mr. Johnson's experience with

large orchestras has given him unusual
knowledge of instrumentation. Carl Diton,
organist and pianist, has so far been interested chiefly in the transcription of Negro
melodies for the organ. "Swing Low, Sweet
Chariot" was published by Schirmer and followed by "Four Jubilee Songs." Clarence
Cameron White, the violinist, has also entered the ranks of the composers with "Ban-
danna Sketches" and other productions; and
H. Laurence Freeman, now of New York,
composer of several operas using Negro
themes, has waited for only a favorable com-
bination of circumstances to give critical and
popular approval to his very excellent work.
Of the men who are just beginning their
careers, E. H. Margetson, organist of the
Chapel of the Crucifixion, New York, and
J. Harold Brown, of Indianapolis, are among
the more promising. The race and the whole
world of music suffered signal loss a few
years ago in the death of Edmund T. Jenkins,
of Charleston, S. C., who made his way to the
Royal Academy in London. Already able to
perform on half a dozen instruments, this
young man was soon awarded a scholarship;

in 1916-17 he was awarded a silver medal for excellence on the clarinet, a bronze medal for his work on the piano, and, against brilliant competition, a second prize for his original work in composition. The year also witnessed the production of his "Prélude Réligieuse" at one of the grand orchestral concerts of the Academy.

Outstanding among the pianists is Hazel Harrison, now of New York. This artist has been to Germany for prolonged periods of study, and she now exhibits complete command of her chosen instrument. Her programs regularly include some of the more difficult compositions of Liszt; recently she has emphasized the new color music; and the power of her performance is frequently such as to thrill the heart of an audience. Raymond Augustus Lawson conducts at Hartford one of the leading studios in New England. His technique is very highly developed, and he has more than once been a soloist at the concerts of the Hartford Philharmonic Orchestra, and appeared on other notable occasions. He has also had the pleasure of seeing different ones of his students

pass on to important places in the musical
life of the country. While such artists as
these can not possibly be overlooked, there
are, after them, so many excellent pianists
that even a most competent and well-informed
musician would hesitate before passing judgment upon them. Among the organists one
thinks quickly of William Herbert Bush, for
years at the Second Congregational Church,
New London, Conn., and of Frederick P.
White, for years at the First Methodist
Episcopal Church, Charlestown, Mass. Mel-
ville Charlton, of Brooklyn, an associate of
the American Guild of Organists, has now
won for himself a place among the foremost
organists in the United States, and he has
also done good work as a composer. He has
been earnestly devoted to his art, and from
him may not unreasonably be expected many
years of exalted endeavor. Excellent vio-
linists are numerous. Foremost is Clarence
Cameron White, well known throughout the
country for his pleasing work. Also prominent in recent years have been Joseph Douglass, of Washington, and Kemper Harreld,
of Atlanta. In this general sketch of those

who have added to the musical achievement
of the race there is a name that must not be
overlooked. "Blind Tom," who attracted so
much attention a generation ago, deserves
notice as a prodigy rather than as a musician
of solid achievement. His real name was
Thomas Bethune, and he was born in Colum-
bus, Ga., in 1849. He was peculiarly sus-
ceptible to the influences of nature, and
imitated on the piano all the sounds he knew.
Without being able to read a note he could
play from memory the most difficult compositions of Beethoven and Mendelssohn. In
phonetics he was especially skillful. Before
his audiences he would commonly invite any
of his hearers to play new and difficult selections, and as soon as a rendering was finished
he would himself play the composition without making a single mistake.

Of those who have exhibited the capabilities of the Negro voice in song it is but
natural that sopranos should have been most
distinguished. Even before the Civil War
the race produced one of the first rank in
Elizabeth Taylor Greenfield, who came into
prominence in 1851. This artist, born in

Mississippi, was taken to Philadelphia and there cared for by a Quaker lady. Said *The Daily State Register,* of Albany, after one of her concerts: "The compass of her marvelous voice embraces twenty-seven notes, reaching from the sonorous bass of a baritone to a few notes above even Jenny Lind's highest." A voice with a range of more than three octaves naturally attracted much attention in both England and America, and comparisons with Jenny Lind, then at the height of her fame, were frequent. After her success on the stage Elizabeth Greenfield became a teacher of music in Philadelphia. Twenty-five years later the Hyers Sisters, Anna and Emma, of San Francisco, started on their memorable tour of the continent, winning some of their greatest triumphs in critical New England. Anna Hyers especially was remarked as a phenomenon. Then rose Madame Selika, a cultured singer of the first rank, and one who, by her arias and operatic work generally, as well as by her mastery of language, won great success on the Continent of Europe as well as in England and America. The careers of two later singers are so recent as to be still fresh in the public memory. It was in 1887 that Flora Batson entered on the period of her greatest success. She was a ballad singer and her work at its best was of the sort that sends an audience into the wildest enthusiasm. Her voice exhibited a compass of three octaves, from the purest, most clear-cut soprano, sweet and full, to the rich round notes of the baritone register. Three or four years later than Flora Batson in her period of greatest artistic success was Sissieretta Jones. The voice of this singer, when it first attracted wide attention, about 1893, commanded notice as one of unusual richness and volume, and as one exhibiting especially the plaintive quality ever present in the typical Negro voice.

In this general review mention must be made of a remarkable company of singers who first made the folk-songs of the race known to the world at large. In 1871 the Fisk Jubilee Singers began their memorable progress through America and Europe, meeting at first with scorn and sneers, but before long touching the heart of the world with their strange music. The original band consisted of four young men and five young women; in the seven years of the existence of the company altogether twenty-four persons were enrolled in it. These singers raised for Fisk University not less than one hundred and fifty thousand dollars, and secured school books, paintings, and apparatus to the value of seven or eight thousand more. They sang in the United States, England, Scotland, Ireland, Holland, Switzerland, and Germany, sometimes before royalty. Since their time they have been much imitated, but hardly ever equaled, and never surpassed.

At the present time Harry T. Burleigh instantly commands attention. For more than twenty-five years he has been the baritone soloist at St. George's Episcopal Church, New York, and for nearly as long at Temple Emanu-El, the synagogue on Fifth Avenue. As a concert and oratorio singer he has met with signal success. Mme. Florence Cole Talbert, winner of a diamond medal at Chicago in 1916, has been outstanding in concert work in recent years; Mme. Anita Patti Brown, a product of the Chicago conservatories, has delighted many audiences by the sympathetic quality of her singing; and Marian Anderson, of Philadelphia, has taken rank as a prominent contralto. Mrs. Maud Cuney Hare, of Boston, a concert pianist, has elicited much favorable comment from cultured persons by her lecture-recitals dealing with Afro-American music as well as by her special articles in the representative musical magazines.

The career of one singer, not yet mentioned, is unique even in the remarkable annals of the stage.

Roland Hayes was born in 1887 in an humble home near Curryville, Ga., fifty miles from Chattanooga. His father died when he was twelve years old, but long before that had been badly hurt when a great log fell on him, so that the boy's mother had to plough or hoe for hours and then come back to the house to cook and wash and iron. When Roland was fifteen years old the family, seeing no future in Curryville, moved to Chattanooga, and there the gifted boy found a job in a factory that made paper weights. He had to unload pig iron, handle the rough scrap iron, charge the cupolas with wood,

coke, and iron, and carry heavy ladles brim-
ming with melted ore. Sometimes the flakes
of liquid metal would fall and burn his feet.
For such service he was paid eighty cents a
day. Later he became a core maker in the
factory. Meanwhile he sang in a little church
choir, and at seventeen he met Arthur Calhoun, a young man who had studied at
Oberlin and who was teaching in Chattanooga. Then came the first of the great
spiritual experiences of the future singer.
One night Calhoun took him to the home of
a white man of the city who was interested in
music; the boy sang; and before the evening
was over the host played for him records of
Caruso, Sembrich, and other artists. "That
night," he said later, "I was born again. It
was as if a bell had been struck, that rang in
my heart. And it has never ceased to ring
there! I had not known what my friend
meant when he talked of music. I had not
been capable of imagining it. The revelation
was so overwhelming that I was like one who
has been born blind and suddenly is given
sight."

Before long came an opportunity to work

ROLAND HAYES

with the Fisk Singers, who were making a
special trip to Boston, and, through the efforts of Mr. Henry H. Putnam, the young
man became a pupil of Arthur Hubbard. He
took his mother to Boston, and after a
while came the first of many appearances in
Symphony Hall. Then came another great
experience, a second rebirth. One night in
California a man said to him that there was
something in his singing that was not in that
of white artists, and asked him what it was.
"What did I know of myself, of my people?" he asked when alone with himself.
"Here we are in America. We were lifted
out of our old environment and set down
here—aliens in body and in soul. Shreds
and tatters of our ancient qualities still cling
to us even now; but what was the original
fabric like?"

He wanted to go to Africa, perhaps to
learn the secret of it all. The world, however, was unsettled after the war, and he
lingered in England. There the Negro was
not very popular at the moment; nevertheless the way was cleared, and on May 31, 1920,
Roland Hayes gave the first of many recitals

in London. His career since then has been
one of the romances of the history of music.

He has appeared before the King and
Queen of England, and received a special
token from the sovereign. In New York he
has filled Carnegie Hall again and again,
singing amid the greatest enthusiasm. Under
the Boston Symphony management he has
toured Europe and America, making all audiences wonder at the spell cast by his voice.
By his culture and his art alike he has done
credit to the people whom he has represented.

Said the *Pravda* of Moscow after one of his
concerts: "The début of Roland Hayes had
to be the greatest event of the musical world
of to-day, and truly it has proved itself the
greatest. . . . Out of every song with its
deeply musical mood was born a feeling of
wonder reaching such a high point in technique that we can speak of it only with the
highest praise. The voice of Hayes does not
belong to the strong or brilliant type, his
voice is rather soft-hued for a tenor, perhaps
not even vivid for his highest notes. He is
typically the lyric singer, lacking the strongly
pathetic tones but capable at the same time

of causing his hearers to experience just what
he feels. Everything coarse or rude and
affected is entirely strange to his artistic
nature. The thoughtful and sweet Schubert
or the mighty Brahms, the indisputably good
Italian arias, the sad humor of the Negro
hymns, he gives them all in such a way that
every moment one forgets about the artist as
interpreter who comes between the audience
and the song.''

With all of the success, however, the singer
himself has grown more modest, more unaffected, more conscious of a divine mission in
his art. ''If, as I truly believe,'' he says,
''there is purpose and plan in my life, it is
this: that I shall help my people to *use* what
has been given to them; that I shall have my
share in rediscovering the qualities we have
almost let slip away from us; and that we
shall make our special contribution—only an
humble one perhaps, but our very own!—to
human experience.''

We could not close on a better note than
that. What Mr. Hayes has said might well
speak for all the writers and artists men-

tioned in this book. With them in a very real sense art has a mission. Never can they forget that they are part of a struggling people, waiting for the full coming of the Kingdom. Phillis Wheatley, Paul L. Dunbar, Henry O. Tanner, Charles Gilpin, and Harry T. Burleigh have wrought well. Sometimes they have waited long for recognition. Sometimes the gleam that led them on has turned to a wintry glimmer. Through all heart-breaking circumstance, however, they have held to an inner light. Their ideals have conquered life's difficulties. Let us hope that those who come after may be worthy of the great tradition.

APPENDIX

1. THE NEGRO IN AMERICAN FICTION

EVER since Sydney Smith sneered at American books a hundred years ago, honest critics have asked themselves if the literature of the United States was not really open to the charge of provincialism. Within the last year or two the argument has been very much revived; and an English critic, Mr. Edward Garnett, writing in *The Atlantic Monthly*, has pointed out that with our predigested ideas and made-to-order fiction we not only discourage individual genius, but make it possible for the multitude to think only such thoughts as have passed through a sieve. Our most popular novelists, and sometimes our most respectable writers, see only the sensation that is uppermost for the moment in the mind of the crowd—divorce, graft, tainted meat or money—and they proceed to cut the cloth of their fiction accordingly. Mr. Owen Wister, a "regular practitioner" of the novelist's art, in substance admitting the weight of these charges, lays the blame on our crass democracy which utterly refuses to do its own thinking and which is satisfied only with the tinsel and gewgaws and hobbyhorses of literature. And no theme has suffered so much from the coarseness of the mob-spirit in literature as that of the Negro.

As a matter of fact, the Negro in his problems

and strivings offers to American writers the greatest opportunity that could possibly be given to them to-day. It is commonly agreed that only one other large question, that of the relations of capital and labor, is of as much interest to the American public; and even this great issue fails to possess quite the appeal offered by the Negro from the social standpoint. One can only imagine what a Victor Hugo, detached and philosophical, would have done with such a theme in a novel. When we see what actually has been done—how often in the guise of fiction a writer has preached a sermon or shouted a political creed, or vented his spleen— we are not exactly proud of the art of novel-writing as it has been developed in the United States of America. Here was opportunity for tragedy, for comedy, for the subtle portrayal of all the relations of man with his fellow man, for faith and hope and love and sorrow. And yet, with the Civil War fifty years in the distance, not one novel or one short story of the first rank has found its inspiration in this great theme. Instead of such work we have consistently had traditional tales, political tracts, and lurid melodramas.

Let us see who have approached the theme, and just what they have done with it, for the present leaving out of account all efforts put forth by Negro writers themselves.

The names of four exponents of Southern life come at once to mind—George W. Cable, Joel Chandler Harris, Thomas Nelson Page, and Thomas Dixon; and at once, in their outlook and method of work, the first two become separate from the last two. Cable and Harris have looked toward the past, and have embalmed vanished or vanishing types. Mr. Page and Mr. Dixon, with their thought on the present (though for the most part they portray the recent past), have used the novel as a vehicle for political propaganda.

It was in 1879 that "Old Creole Days" evidenced the advent of a new force in American literature; and on the basis of this work, and of "The Grandissimes" which followed, Mr. Cable at once took his place as the foremost portrayer of life in old New Orleans. By birth, by temperament, and by training he was thoroughly fitted for the task to which he set himself. His mother was from New England, his father of the stock of colonial Virginia; and the stern Puritanism of the North was mellowed by the gentler influences of the South. Moreover, from his long apprenticeship in newspaper work in New Orleans he had received abundantly the knowledge and training necessary for his work. Setting himself to a study of the Negro of the old régime, he made a specialty of the famous—and infamous—quadroon society of Louisiana of the third and fourth decades of the last century. And excellent as was his work, turning his face to the past in manner as well as in matter, from the very first he raised the question propounded by this paper. In his earliest volume there was a story entitled "'Tite Poulette," the heroine of which was a girl amazingly fair, the supposed daughter of one Madame John. A young Dutchman fell in love with 'Tite Poulette, championed her cause at all times, suffered a beating and stabbing for her,

and was by her nursed back to life and love. In
the midst of his perplexity about joining himself
to a member of another race, came the word from
Madame John that the girl was not her daughter,
but the child of yellow fever patients whom she
had nursed until they died, leaving their infant in
her care. Immediately upon the publication of
this story, the author received a letter from a young
woman who had actually lived in very much the
same situation as that portrayed in "'Tite Poulette," telling him that his story was not true to
life and that he knew it was not, for Madame
John really *was* the mother of the heroine. Accept-
ing the criticism, Mr. Cable set about the composition of "Madame Delphine," in which the situation
is somewhat similar, but in which at the end the
mother tamely makes a confession to a priest.
What is the trouble? The artist is so bound by
circumstances and hemmed in by tradition that he
simply has not the courage to launch out into the
deep and work out his human problems for himself.
Take a representative portrait from "The Grandissimes":

Clemence had come through ages of African savagery,
through fires that do not refine, but that blunt and blast
and blacken and char; starvation, gluttony, drunken-
ness, thirst, drowning, nakedness, dirt, fetichism, de-
bauchery, slaughter, pestilence, and the rest—she was
their heiress; they left her the cinders of human feelings.
... She had had children of assorted colors—had one with
her now, the black boy that brought the basil to Joseph;
the others were here and there, some in the Grandissime
households or field-gangs, some elsewhere within occasional

sight, some dead, some not accounted for. Husbands—
like the Samaritan woman's. We know she was a constant singer and laugher.

Very brilliant of course; and yet Clemence is a
relic, not a prophecy.

Still more of a relic is Uncle Remus. For decades
now, this charming old Negro has been held up
to the children of the South as the perfect expression
of the beauty of life in the glorious times "befo'
de wah," when every Southern gentleman was
suckled at the bosom of a "black mammy." Why
should we not occasionally attempt to paint the
Negro of the new day—intelligent, ambitious,
thrifty, manly? Perhaps he is not so poetic; but
certainly the human element is greater.

To the school of Cable and Harris belong also
of course Miss Grace King and Mrs. Ruth McEnery
Stuart, a thoroughly representative piece of work
being Mrs. Stuart's "Uncle 'Riah's Christmas Eve."
Other more popular writers of the day, Miss Mary
Johnston and Miss Ellen Glasgow for instance,
attempt no special analysis of the Negro. They
simply take him for granted as an institution that
always has existed and always will exist, as a hewer
of wood and drawer of water, from the first flush
of creation to the sounding of the trump of doom.

But more serious is the tone when we come to
Thomas Nelson Page and Thomas Dixon. We
might tarry for a few minutes with Mr. Page to
listen to more such tales as those of Uncle Remus;
but we must turn to living issues. Times have
changed. The grandson of Uncle Remus does not

feel that he must stand with his hat in his hand when he is in our presence, and he even presumes to help us in the running of our government. This will never do; so in "Red Rock" and "The Leopard's Spots" it must be shown that he should never have been allowed to vote anyway, and those honorable gentlemen in the Congress of the United States in the year 1865 did not know at all what they were about. Though we are given the characters and setting of a novel, the real business is to show that the Negro has been the "sentimental pet" of the nation all too long. By all means let us have an innocent white girl, a burly Negro, and a burning at the stake, or the story would be incomplete.

We have the same thing in "The Clansman," a "drama of fierce revenge." But here we are concerned very largely with the blackening of a man's character. Stoneman (Thaddeus Stevens very thinly disguised) is himself the whole Congress of the United States. He is a gambler, and "spends a part of almost every night at Hall & Pemberton's Faro Place on Pennsylvania Avenue." He is hysterical, "drunk with the joy of a triumphant vengeance." "The South is conquered soil," he says to the President (a mere figure-head, by the way), "I mean to blot it from the map." Further: "It is but the justice and wisdom of heaven that the Negro shall rule the land of his bondage. It is the only solution of the race problem. Wait until I put a ballot in the hand of every Negro, and a bayonet at the breast of every white man from the James to the Rio Grande." Stoneman, moreover, has a mistress, a mulatto woman, a "yellow vampire" who dominates him completely. "Senators, representatives, politicians of low and high degree, artists, correspondents, foreign ministers, and cabinet officers hurried to acknowledge their fealty to the uncrowned king, and hail the strange brown woman who held the keys of his house as the first lady of the land." This, let us remember, was for some months the best-selling book in the United States. A slightly altered version of it has very recently commanded such prices as were never before paid for seats at a moving-picture entertainment; and with "The Traitor" and "The Southerner" it represents our most popular treatment of the gravest social question in American life! "The Clansman" is to American literature exactly what a Louisiana mob is to American democracy. Only too frequently, of course, the mob represents us all too well.

Turning from the longer works of fiction to the short story, I have been interested to see how the matter has been dealt with here. For purposes of comparison I have selected from ten representative periodicals as many distinct stories, no one of which was published more than ten years ago; and as these are in almost every case those stories that first strike the eye in a periodical index, we may assume that they are thoroughly typical. The ten are: "Shadow," by Harry Stillwell Edwards, in the *Century* (December, 1906); "Callum's Co'tin': A Plantation Idyl," by Frank H. Sweet, in the *Craftsman* (March, 1907); "His Excellency the Governor," by L. M. Cooke, in *Putnam's* (Febru-

ary, 1908); "The Black Drop," by Margaret De-
land in *Collier's Weekly* (May 2 and 9, 1908);
"Jungle Blood," by Elmore Elliott Peake, in *Mc-
Clure's* (September, 1908); "The Race-Rioter," by
Harris Merton Lyon, in the *American* (February,
1910); "Shadow," by Grace MacGowan Cooke
and Alice MacGowan, in *Everybody's* (March,
1910); "Abram's Freedom," by Edna Turpin, in
the *Atlantic* (September, 1912); "A Hypothetical
Case," by Norman Duncan, in *Harper's* (June,
1915); and "The Chalk Game," by L. B. Yates, in
the *Saturday Evening Post* (June 5, 1915). For
high standards of fiction I think we may safely
say that, all in all, the periodicals here mentioned
are representative of the best that America has to
offer. In some cases the story cited is the only one
on the Negro question that a magazine has published within the decade.

"Shadow" (in the *Century*) is the story of a Negro
convict who for a robbery committed at the age
of fourteen was sentenced to twenty years of hard
labor in the mines of Alabama. An accident dis-
abled him, however, and prevented his doing the
regular work for the full period of his imprisonment.
At twenty he was a hostler, looking forward in
despair to the fourteen years of confinement still
waiting for him. But the three little girls of the
prison commissioner visit the prison. Shadow per-
forms many little acts of kindness for them, and
their hearts go out to him. They storm the governor
and the judge for his pardon, and present the Negro
with his freedom as a Christmas gift. The story is
not long, but it strikes a note of genuine pathos.

"Callum's Co'tin'" is concerned with a hard-working Negro, a blacksmith, nearly forty, who goes courting the girl who called at his shop to get a trinket mended for her mistress. At first he makes himself ridiculous by his finery; later he makes the mistake of coming to a crowd of merrymakers in his working clothes. More and more, however, he storms the heart of the girl, who eventually capitulates. From the standpoint simply of crafts-manship, the story is an excellent piece of work.

"His Excellency the Governor" deals with the custom on Southern plantations of having, in imi-tation of the white people, a Negro "governor" whose duty it was to settle minor disputes. At the death of old Uncle Caleb, who for years had held this position of responsibility, his son Jubal should have been the next in order. He was likely to be superseded, however, by loud-mouthed Sambo, though urged to assert himself by Maria, his wife, an old house-servant who had no desire whatever to be defeated for the place of honor among the women by Sue, a former field-hand. At the meeting where all was to be decided, however, Jubal with the aid of his fiddle completely confounded his rival and won. There are some excellent touches in the story; but, on the whole, the composition is hardly more than fair in literary quality.

"The Black Drop," throughout which we see the hand of an experienced writer, analyzes the heart of a white boy who is in love with a girl who is almost white, and who when the test confronts him suffers the tradition that binds him to get the better of his heart. "But you will still believe that

I love you?" he asks, ill at ease as they separate. "No, of course I can not believe that," replies the girl.

"Jungle Blood" is the story of a simple-minded, simple-hearted Negro of gigantic size who in a moment of fury kills his pretty wife and the white man who has seduced her. The tone of the whole may be gleaned from the description of Moss Harper's father: "An old darky sat drowsing on the stoop. There was something ape-like about his long arms, his flat, wide-nostriled nose, and the mat of gray wool which crept down his forehead to within two inches of his eyebrows."

"The Race-Rioter" sets forth the stand of a brave young sheriff to protect his prisoner, a Negro boy, accused of the assault and murder of a little white girl. Hank Egge tries by every possible subterfuge to defeat the plans of a lynching party, and finally dies riddled with bullets as he is defending his prisoner. The story is especially remarkable for the strong and sympathetic characterization of such contrasting figures as young Egge and old Dikeson, the father of the dead girl.

"Shadow" (in *Everybody's*) is a story that depends for its force very largely upon incident. It studies the friendship of a white boy, Ranny, and a black boy, Shadow, a relationship that is opposed by both the Northern white mother and the ambitious and independent Negro mother. In a fight, Shad breaks a collar-bone for Ranny; later he saves him from drowning. In the face of Ranny's white friends, all the harsher side of the problem is seen; and yet the human element is strong beneath it all. The story, not without considerable merit as it is, would have been infinitely stronger if the friendship of the two boys had been pitched on a higher plane. As it is, Shad is very much like a dog following his master.

"Abram's Freedom" is at the same time one of the most clever and one of the most provoking stories with which we have to deal. It is a perfect example of how one may walk directly up to the light and then deliberately turn his back upon it. The story is set just before the Civil War. It deals with the love of the slave Abram for a free young woman, Emmeline. "All his life he had heard and used the phrase 'free nigger' as a term of contempt. What, then, was this vague feeling, not definite enough yet to be a wish or even a longing?" So far, so good. Emmeline inspires within her lover the highest ideals of manhood, and he becomes a hostler in a livery-stable, paying to his master so much a year for his freedom. Then comes the astounding and forced conclusion. At the very moment when, after years of effort, Emmeline has helped her husband to gain his freedom (and when all the slaves are free as a matter of fact by virtue of the Emancipation Proclamation), Emmeline, whose husband has special reason to be grateful to his former master, says to the lady of the house: "Me an' Abram ain't got nothin' to do in dis worl' but to wait on you an' master."

In "A Hypothetical Case" we again see the hand of a master-craftsman. Is a white boy justified in shooting a Negro who has offended him? The white father is not quite at ease, quibbles a good deal, but finally says Yes. The story, however, makes it clear that the Negro did not strike the boy. He was a hermit living on the Florida coast and perfectly abased when he met Mercer and his two companions. When the three boys pursued him and finally overtook him, the Negro simply held the hands of Mercer until the boy had recovered his temper. Mercer in his rage really struck himself.

"The Chalk Game" is the story of a little Negro jockey who wins a race in Louisville only to be drugged and robbed by some "flashlight" Negroes who send him to Chicago. There he recovers his fortunes by giving to a group of gamblers the correct "tip" on another race, and he makes his way back to Louisville much richer by his visit. Throughout the story emphasis is placed upon the superstitious element in the Negro race, an element readily considered by men who believe in luck.

Of these ten stories, only five strike out with even the slightest degree of independence. "Shadow" (in the *Century*) is not a powerful piece of work, but it is written in tender and beautiful spirit. "The Black Drop" is a bold handling of a strong situation. "The Race-Rioter" also rings true, and in spite of the tragedy there is optimism in this story of a man who is not afraid to do his duty. "Shadow" (in *Everybody's*) awakens all sorts of discussion, but at least attempts to deal honestly with a situation that might arise in any neighborhood at any time. "A Hypothetical Case" is the most tense and independent story in the list. On the other hand, "Callum's Co'tin'" and

"His Excellency the Governor," bright comedy though they are, belong, after all, to the school of Uncle Remus. "Jungle Blood" and "The Chalk Game" belong to the class that always regards the Negro as an animal, a minor, a plaything—but never as a man. "Abram's Freedom," exceedingly well written for two-thirds of the way, falls down hopelessly at the end. Many old Negroes after the Civil War preferred to remain with their former masters; but certainly no young woman of the type of Emmeline would sell her birthright for a mess of pottage.

Just there is the point. That the Negro is ever to be taken seriously is incomprehensible to some people. It is the story of "The Man that Laughs" over again. The more Gwynplaine protests, the more outlandish he becomes to the House of Lords.

We are simply asking that those writers of fiction who deal with the Negro shall be thoroughly honest with themselves, and not remain forever content to embalm old types and work over outworn ideas. Rather should they sift the present and forecast the future. But of course the editors must be considered. The editors must give their readers what the readers want; and when we consider the populace, of course we have to reckon with the mob. And the mob does not find anything very attractive about a Negro who is intelligent, cultured, manly, and who does not smile. It will be observed that in no one of the ten stories above mentioned, not even in one of the five remarked most favorably, is there a Negro of this type. Yet he is obliged to come. America has yet to reckon with him. The day of Uncle Remus as well as of Uncle Tom is over.

Even now, however, there are signs of better things. Such an artist as Mr. Howells, for instance, has once or twice dealt with the problem in excellent spirit. Then there is the work of the Negro writers themselves. The numerous attempts in fiction made by them have most frequently been open to the charge of crassness already considered; but Paul Laurence Dunbar, Charles W. Chesnutt, and W. E. Burghardt DuBois have risen above the crowd. Mr. Dunbar, of course, was better in poetry than in prose. Such a short story as "Jimsella," however, exhibited considerable technique. "The Uncalled" used a living topic treated with only partial success. But for the most part, Mr. Dunbar's work looked toward the past. Somewhat stronger in prose is Mr. Chesnutt. "The Marrow of Tradition" is not much more than a political tract, and "The Colonel's Dream" contains a good deal of preaching; but "The House Behind the Cedars" is a real novel. Among his short stories, "The Bouquet" may be remarked for technical excellence, and "The Wife of His Youth" for a situation of unusual power. Dr. DuBois's "The Quest of the Silver Fleece" contains at least one strong [dramatic situation, that in which Bles probes the heart of Zora; but the author is a sociologist and essayist rather than a novelist. The grand epic of the race is yet to be produced.

Some day we shall work out the problems of our great country. Some day we shall not have a state government set at defiance, and the massacre

of Ludlow. Some day our little children will not
slave in mines and mills, but will have some chance
at the glory of God's creation; and some day the
Negro will cease to be a problem and become a
human being. Then, in truth, we shall have the
Promised Land. But until that day comes let
those who mold our ideals and set the standards
of our art in fiction at least be honest with themselves and independent. Ignorance we may for a
time forgive; but a man has only himself to blame
if he insists on not seeing the sunrise in the new
day.

2. THE NEGRO IN AMERICAN LITERATURE

(From an article with this title in *The Bookman,*
October, 1922)

I HAVE often wondered why someone has not
written as a supplement to Lowell an essay
entitled "On a Certain Condescension in Americans." Such an effort, in some small measure at
least, might serve to give us a clearer estimate of
ourselves.

When the drums beat we are not likely to recall
that we are the most inconsistent people in the
world. We pride ourselves on spending millions
for education, but the draft showed us where we
stood, and we have recently been informed that we
are merely a nation of sixth-graders. We still
value buildings more than brains, and if you will
ask the average college student to read aloud a page
of Newman or Pater you will see how literate we
are. We are aghast at Armenia—naturally, for in
Texas we lynch ten men in twice as many days.

We have been accused of intolerance, and a
finger has been pointed at the Puritan. As a matter of fact we are exceedingly long suffering. We
tolerate everything from sixteen dollar coal to our
most recent Congress. We tolerate the Ku Klux
Klan. A score of men were killed in Herrin in cold
blood, and the authorities are paralyzed. For a
sensible liberty loving people we are the most

easily browbeaten and bamboozled on this planet, and no one knows this better than the politician.

* * * * *

Our inconsistency does not mean that as a nation we have lost sight of our port. It does mean, however, that we wander needlessly at sea before finding it. Democracy does not always move in a straight line, and sometimes when far off its course it has to make a violent effort to find its way. While moreover we talk about democracy, the fact is that there are always with us those who want something else. In the good old days Rhode Island was the most offensive little slave dealer in the country, and we do not always stop to think that there was a time when the students at Harvard were registered in the catalogue on the basis of their social standing. Among the rockribbed families of Boston there was ever a welcome for the courtly Southerner with whom trade was good and behind whom was the romance of plantations and slaves. It is not an accident that in recent discussion of the Jew and the Negro New England has again beckoned to the South. Sooner or later in such a civilization the worm turns; the underdog wriggles out of our grasp; and, the glory of democracy is that it gives him a chance to work out his freedom—and live.

In the new day to which we have come it is necessary first of all then that we keep our faith— faith in our country, in ourselves, in humanity. Let us also as never before honor Truth—not propaganda, not the flattery of a demagogue, and not the jaundice of a hectic journalism, but simple,

clear-eyed Truth. This will mean that we shall
have to readjust many old values and beware of
all outgrown shibboleths. Our country is chang-
ing, and those persons who insist on abiding by the
opinions formed twenty years ago simply insist on
living in another age and another world.

With nothing shall we have to be more careful
about hasty judgment than with subjects relating
to the Negro. To-day there is no telling what an
individual Negro may or may not do. At the close
of the Civil War hardly more than one in ten could
read; to-day illiteracy has been reduced to nearly
twenty per cent, and instead of his being your
tenant you may even find that the Negro you know
is your landlord. The race is increasingly complex,
and in some matters of music and other forms of
art it is just now among the most "advanced" in
the country. The Negro is naturally such an
artist and he has such an innate appreciation of
acting that, keeping his essential faith unchanged,
he is likely to take on a new form of worship quite
as easily as a new garment. Just now Bahaism is
popular with the esoteric, and since the war cyni-
cism has been developed almost to a cult.

This, however, is only one phase of the matter.
The other is that of the strange prominence of the
Negro throughout the whole course of American
history. In the colonial era it was the economic
advantage of slavery over servitude that caused it
to displace this institution as a system of labor.
Two of the three compromises that entered into the
making of the Constitution were prompted by the
presence of the Negro in the country; the expan-

sion of the Southwest depended on his labor; and the question of the excuse of fugitives was the real key to the Seminole Wars. The Civil War was simply to determine the status of the Negro in the Republic, and the legislation after the war determined for a generation the history not only of the South but very largely of the nation as well. The later disfranchising acts have had overwhelming importance, the unfair system of national representation controlling the election of 1916 and thus the attitude of America in the World War.

Here then are two great themes—that of the Negro's aspiration and striving, and that of his influence on the American body politic—that might reasonably engage the attention of any writer who desires seriously to base a contribution to American literature on this general topic. The first would call for treatment primarily subjective, the second for treatment largely objective; but in any case the work should be sympathetic in the broadest sense. Such treatment I regret the Negro has not had. With our bigotry and conceit, on this subject as no other we have been moved by the condescension of which I spoke in the beginning. Two great fallacies still most frequently recur as major premises. One is that the education of the Negro has been a failure, and the other is that the integrity of the womanhood of the race is always open to question. It makes no difference how much evidence there may be to the contrary, any writer of the day is still likely to start off with these two assumptions. The Negro himself moreover must be either a brute or a villain; no rôle more flattering can be thought of. "Othello" is not yet a popular play with American audiences, and I cannot help recalling that some years ago a Shakesperian company performing "The Merchant of Venice" in Atlanta found it advisable to leave out even the Prince of Morocco, because of local conditions.

Literature is supposed to be the reflection of the national life. Unfortunately much of our recent literature is not complimentary to the country's life. We have the best printers and publishers in the world, but the books that they are asked to produce—tales of scandal sicklied o'er with sentimentalism—should make the nation blush. A generation ago people smiled at E. P. Roe; but Roe was at least harmless. More recently we have arrived at Harold Bell Wright, but even he has been out-Heroded. If we to-day go over the list of writers of fiction—especially the women—and consider only those who are outstanding, the extent to which many will be found to have declined from the ideals with which they started is astonishing. In all this welter of commercialism and sensationalism the Negro's one request of literature so far as he is concerned, is that it be fearlessly and absolutely honest. Let it portray life, realistically —just as it is, idealistically—as it ought to be,— but let it cease to exploit outworn theories or be the vehicle merely of burlesque. A new age—a new world—is upon us, with new men, new visions, new desires. As never before patriotism demands that we see life clearly and see it whole.

It is now a little more than six years ago that I

contributed to "The Dial" (then in Chicago) a
paper entitled "The Negro in American Fiction."
In that discussion I endeavored to deal at some
length with the work of several authors—notably
George W. Cable, Joel Chandler Harris, Thomas
Nelson Page, and Thomas Dixon—as well as with
that of representative short story writers of the
day who had introduced Negro characters into their
work. In general I advanced the proposition that
in our literature as in our social life we were
largely dominated by the mob spirit. Much has
happened within six years, and now that the war
is four years behind us and we are trying to find
the "normalcy" of which we have heard, we may
not unreasonably ask if there has been any advance. At once we come face to face with the
stories and sketches of E. K. Means and Octavus
Roy Cohen, and these we find to be burlesque.
Five other works of fiction also come to mind, however—"His Own Country" by Paul Kester, "The
Shadow" by Mary White Ovington, "Birthright"
by T. S. Stribling, "White and Black" by H. A.
Shands, and "J. Poindexter, Colored" by Irwin S.
Cobb. The last three of these books, it is interesting to observe, have all appeared within the present
year, and practically every one of the five is, if not
the only book, at least the first novel by its author.
Taken together these books mark an advance, but
one would hardly assert that they give an adequate
reflection of the Negro problem in a treatment
at once faithful, powerful, and tragic. "The
Shadow," is honest in purpose and method. "His
Own Country" and "White and Black," however,

while containing much of the machinery of tragedy, both fail to be genuine epics. "Birthright," brilliant in some of its details, begs the whole question with which it undertakes to deal by its attitude on fundamentals, and the treatment of its hero is especially open to attack. J. Poindexter, of Paducah, who awakens our interest and who is so thoroughly equal to the wiles and pitfalls of New York, himself advises us not to bother with the race problem. "I ain't no problem, I's a pusson," he says; "I craves to be so reguarded." To that extent he marks an advance.

* * * * *

Literature should be not only history but prophecy, not only the record of our striving but also the mirror of our hopes and dreams. Let us have the forward as well as the backward look. In England we speak of the Liberalism of Lloyd George as distinct from the old Liberalism of Gladstone. Some such distinction needs to be made in our own country. The disfranchisement of any number or group of citizens, real or attempted, in the United States of America in the third decade of the twentieth century, is an anachronism. We may try to turn back the clock, but the hands of Time move inexorably forward. Let us be worthy of the new day.

The Negro himself as the irony of American civilization is the supreme challenge to American literature. Like Banquo's ghost he will not down. All faith and hope, all love and longing, all rapture and despair, look out from the eyes of this man who is ever with us and whom we never understand. Gentle as a child, he has also the strength of Hercules. The more we think we know him the more unfathomable he is. No wonder a well known senator who maligned the Negro felt that he was paralyzed because the race prayed that God might afflict him. No wonder is it that, submerged, the Negro still rises from the depths to cast by his magic an irresistible spell over the American mind.

3. THE NEGRO IN CONTEMPORARY LITERATURE

(From an article with this title in *The English Journal,* March, 1929)

THE books that have been written by white people within the last eight years range all the way from first-hand studies of elemental Negro life to formal novels, such a sophisticated piece of writing as Vandercook's popular *Black Majesty,* and such a ponderous study as Puckett's *Folk Beliefs of the Southern Negro.* The studies in folk-lore and the reproductions of simple or peasant life would include the following: *The Black Border* and *With Æsop Along the Black Border,* by Ambrose E. Gonzales; *Congaree Sketches* and *Nigger to Nigger,* by E. C. L. Adams; *Black Cameos* and *Gritny People,* by R. Emmett Kennedy; *Rainbow Round My Shoulder,* by Howard W. Odum; and *Ol' Man Adam an' His Chillun,* by Roark Bradford. The first four of these books are set in the lowlands of South Carolina, and they represent faithfully the dialect and superstitions of the untutored Negroes in that part of the world, as well as much of their inheritance from slavery. Keeping their eyes fixed on the subject, they deal little in exposition and let their matter speak for itself, so that they offer material for literature rather than literature itself. Over all broods an air of fatalism.

Mr. Kennedy is concerned with the lowlands of Louisiana, and among the people whom he portrays primitive passion blazes into ardent flame. *Rainbow Round My Shoulder* is the Odyssey of a black Ulysses who wanders from one construction camp to another, from state to state, from wife to wife, and who more than once is sent to the chaingang. *Ol' Man Adam an' His Chillun* is the version by an ignorant preacher of more than thirty stories taken from the Bible. The work is bright at times, but it is greatly exaggerated, and on the whole is burlesque rather than an earnest interpretation of Negro life. Throughout the period that we are considering collections of stories by Octavus Roy Cohen have continued to appear; but the work of this author, as well as that of E. K. Means, today seems wholly to belong to the past. For a while it entertained the readers of the *Saturday Evening Post*, but the caricatures soon became stereotyped and were never to be regarded as literature.

Among the novels significance seems to attach to the following: *Birthright*, by T. S. Stribling; *Nigger*, by Clement Wood; *White and Black*, by H. A. Shands; *Porgy*, by Du Bose Heyward; *Nigger Heaven*, by Carl Van Vechten; and *Black April* and *Scarlet Sister Mary*, by Julia Peterkin. *Birthright* showed considerable sense of literary values, but the hero was both inadequate and unfair as a portrayal of the Negro graduate of Harvard, so that the book could have no abiding value. *Nigger* was not firmly moulded. *Black and White*, set in Texas, suggested situations out of which powerful fiction may be wrought, but was also deficient in organization. *Porgy,* written by a man who is a poet and who is in thorough command of his material, contains passages that are highly sensitive; and the description of the storm in the harbor of Charleston is almost epic in its sweep. *Nigger Heaven,* supposed to be a portrayal of life in Harlem, is a perfect illustration of a book that gives facts but does not tell the truth. Very probably nothing is set down for which the author cannot give the evidence; at the same time the impression that the work gives as a whole is distorted. With the last two books, unless one delights to revel in slime, it is difficult to be patient. One has as its central figure a man and the other a woman on the Blue Brook plantation in South Carolina, both of whom are very light in their love affairs. How far the idea of a novel is worked out may be seen from the fact that in *Black April* one chapter is entitled "Duck-Hunting," the next "The Quilting," and the next "Church," the three having no organic connection whatsoever. The author seems to have kept a notebook in which every coarse speech and every gross emotion of the Negroes who came within her ken was recorded. It is to be regretted that anyone should ever have been thus employed.

It will be observed that this consideration takes no account of books that were written by foreigners or that are set in a foreign land, such as Sarah G. Millin's *God's Step-Children*; nor does it study those in which the Negro is subordinated to another theme, such as Sherwood Anderson's *Dark Laugh-*

ter or Mary Johnston's *The Slave Ship.* Nor have
we so far dealt with the drama. The literature of
the Negro on the stage is now a study in itself, and
only the salient points can be considered here.
After decades of burnt-cork minstrelsy and light
musical comedy, a new era was marked in the
spring of 1914 by the presentation of Ridgely
Torrence's *Granny Maumee,* by the Stage Society
of New York. Here at last was serious drama,
given an auspicious start by the sincere work in the
title rôle of Dorothy Donnelly, one of the most able
actresses of the period. After several other efforts
in the same direction, in the fall of 1920 appeared
Eugene O'Neill's highly successful play, *The Emperor Jones,* which gave opportunity to the Negro
actor, Charles S. Gilpin. A few years later came
the plays of Paul Green dealing with the life of
the Negro in the South. Sometimes the Negro
peasant was portrayed as shouting in religious
frenzy or sunk in sin, sometimes as struggling
against destiny and going down to defeat. In the
spring of 1927 *In Abraham's Bosom* was awarded
the Pulitzer Prize. Such plays as those that have
been mentioned, as well as several by young Negro
writers, are brought together in the collection,
Plays of Negro Life, edited by Alain Locke and
Montgomery Gregory.

There is just one thing to be said about the portrayal of the Negro in literature by persons who
are not members of the race, and that is that there
is undue emphasis on futility and fatalism. It is
significant that several of the books of fiction
mentioned employ in their titles the offensive

word "nigger." The upstanding, industrious, self-respecting Negro who actually succeeds in the battle of life, is not mentioned. Instead there are constantly recurrent the fallacies that the education of the Negro has been a failure and that the integrity of the womanhood of the race is always open to question. No matter how much evidence to the contrary there may be, any author of the day is likely to start out with one or the other of these assumptions. It is very unfortunate that this should be the case.

4. BIBLIOGRAPHY

THE following bibliography is highly eclectic in method. It endeavors to keep constantly in mind the real subject of the present volume, that is, the actual achievement of the Negro in the United States in the fields of literature and art. Books that are mainly experimental or commercial, or that belong primarily to the province of history or sociology, are not mentioned. Nor does the list include general works of fiction that happen to use the Negro as a theme. The more important of these receive at least brief treatment in the preceding sections of the Appendix. Those who desire a more comprehensive list are referred to "The Negro in Contemporary American Literature" (an Outline for Individual and Group Study), by Elizabeth Lay Green, The University of North Carolina Press, Chapel Hill, 1922, and "The New Negro," edited by Alain Locke and published by A. & C. Boni, New York, 1925. The bibliography is in three parts. The first includes only representative works by Negro authors. The second, somewhat more miscellaneous, gives the titles of books critical, biographical, or interpretative, several of which are not by Negroes. The third gives a list of the more important magazine articles that have appeared in recent years.

I

Representative Works by Negro Authors

BRAITHWAITE, WILLIAM STANLEY.

Lyrics of Life and Love. H. B. Turner & Co., Boston, 1904.

The House of Falling Leaves (poems). J. W. Luce & Co., Boston, 1908.

The Book of Elizabethan Verse (anthology). H. B. Turner & Co., Boston, 1906.

The Book of Georgian Verse (anthology). Brentano's, New York, 1908.

The Book of Restoration Verse (anthology). Brentano's, New York, 1909.

Anthology of Magazine Verse for 1913 (including The Magazines and the Poets, a review). Cambridge, Mass., 1913. (This Anthology of Magazine Verse has been issued each year since 1913, most frequently by Small, Maynard & Co., Boston.)

The Poetic Year (for 1916): A Critical Anthology. Small, Maynard & Co., Boston, 1917.

The Golden Treasury of Magazine Verse. Small, Maynard & Co., Boston, 1918.

Victory: Celebrated by Thirty-eight American Poets. Small, Maynard & Co., Boston, 1919.

The Story of the Great War (for young people). Frederick A. Stokes & Co., New York, 1919.

CHESNUTT, CHARLES WADDELL.

Frederick Douglass: A Biography. Small, Maynard & Co., Boston, 1899.

The Conjure Woman (stories). Houghton Mifflin Co., Boston, 1899; new edition, 1929.

The Wife of His Youth, and Other Stories of the Color-line. Houghton Mifflin Co., Boston, 1899.

The House Behind the Cedars (novel). Houghton Mifflin Co., Boston, 1900.

The Marrow of Tradition (novel). Houghton Mifflin Co., Boston, 1901.

The Colonel's Dream (novel). Doubleday, Page & Co., New York, 1905.

COTTER, JOSEPH S., JR.: *The Band of Gideon, and Other Lyrics.* The Cornhill Co., Boston, 1918.

CULLEN, COUNTEE.

Color (poems). Harper & Bros., New York and London, 1925.

Copper Sun (poems). Harper & Bros., New York and London, 1927.

The Ballad of the Brown Girl, an old ballad retold, with illustrations and decorations by Charles Cullen. Harper & Bros., New York and London, 1927.

Caroling Dusk, an Anthology of Verse by Negro Poets (edited), decorations by Aaron Douglas. Harper & Bros., New York and London, 1927.

DUBOIS, WILLIAM EDWARD BURGHARDT.

The Souls of Black Folk: Essays and Sketches. A. C. McClurg & Co., Chicago, 1903.

John Brown (in *American Crisis Biographies*). George W. Jacobs & Co., Philadelphia, 1909.

The Quest of the Silver Fleece (novel). A. C. McClurg & Co., Chicago, 1911.

Darkwater: Voices from Within the Veil. Harcourt, Brace & Co., New York, 1920.

Dark Princess (novel). Harcourt, Brace & Co., New York, 1928.

DUNBAR, PAUL LAURENCE.

Life and Works, edited by Lida Keck Wiggins. J. L. Nichols & Co., Naperville, Ill., 1907.

The following, with the exception of the sketch at the end, were all published by Dodd, Mead & Co., New York.

POEMS:

Lyrics of Lowly Life, 1896.
Lyrics of the Hearthside, 1899.
Lyrics of Love and Laughter, 1903.
Lyrics of Sunshine and Shadow, 1905.
Complete Poems, 1913.

SPECIALLY ILLUSTRATED VOLUMES OF POEMS:

Poems of Cabin and Field, 1899.
Candle-Lightin' Time, 1901.
When Malindy Sings, 1903.
Li'l' Gal, 1904.
Howdy, Honey, Howdy, 1905.
Joggin' Erlong, 1906.
Speakin' o' Christmas, 1914.

NOVELS:

The Uncalled, 1896.
The Love of Landry, 1900.
The Fanatics, 1901.
The Sport of the Gods, 1902.

STORIES AND SKETCHES:

Folks from Dixie, 1898.
The Strength of Gideon, and Other Stories, 1900.
In Old Plantation Days, 1903.

The Heart of Happy Hollow, 1904.

Uncle Eph's Christmas, a one-act musical sketch, Washington, 1900.

DUNBAR, ALICE MOORE (MRS. NELSON).

The Goodness of St. Rocque, and Other Stories. Dodd, Mead & Co., New York, 1899.

Masterpieces of Negro Eloquence (edited). The Bookery Publishing Co., New York, 1914.

FAUSET, JESSIE.

There is Confusion (novel). Boni & Liveright, New York, 1924.

Plum Bun (novel). E. Mathews & Marrot, Ltd., London, 1928; Frederick A. Stokes Co., New York, 1929.

GRIMKÉ, ANGELINA W.: *Rachel* (a play in three acts). The Cornhill Co., Boston, 1920.

HARPER, FRANCES ELLEN WATKINS.

Poems on Miscellaneous Subjects. Boston, 1854, 1856; also Merrihew & Son, Philadelphia, 1857, 1866 (second series), 1871.

Iola Leroy (story). Boston, 1892.

HILL, LESLIE PINCKNEY.

The Wings of Oppression (poems). The Stratford Co., Boston, 1921.

Toussaint L'Ouverture (poem). Christopher Publishing House, Boston, 1928.

HORTON, GEORGE MOSES: *The Hope of Liberty* (poems). Raleigh, N. C., 1929. (Note also *Poems by a Slave,* bound with *Poems of Phillis Wheatley,* Boston, 1838.)

HUGHES, LANGSTON: *The Weary Blues* (poems). Alfred A. Knopf, Inc., New York, 1926.

JOHNSON, GEORGIA DOUGLAS.

  The Heart of a Woman, and Other Poems. The
    Cornhill Co., Boston, 1917.

  Bronze: A Book of Verse. B. J. Brimmer Co.,
    Boston, 1921.

  An Autumn Love Cycle. Harold Vinal, Ltd.,
    New York, 1928.

JOHNSON, FENTON.

  A Little Dreaming (poems). Peterson Lino-
    typing Co., Chicago, 1913.

  Visions of the Dusk (poems). Trachlenburg
    Co., New York, 1915.

  Songs of the Soil. Trachlenburg Co., New York,
    1916.

JOHNSON, JAMES WELDON.

  Autobiography of an Ex-Colored Man (pub-
    lished anonymously). Sherman, French &
    Co., Boston, 1912; new edition, with name on
    title-page and Introduction by Carl Van Vech-
    ten. Alfred A. Knopf, Inc., New York and
    London, 1927.

  Fifty Years, and Other Poems, with Introduction
    by Brander Matthews. The Cornhill Co., Bos-
    ton, 1917; new edition, The Viking Press,
    New York, 1928.

  The Book of American Negro Poetry (edited).
    Harcourt Brace & Co., New York, 1922.

  *God's Trombones: Seven Negro Sermons in
    Verse.* The Viking Press, New York, 1927.

  The Book of American Negro Spirituals (edited
    with Introduction). The Viking Press, New
    York, 1926.

The Second Book of American Negro Spirituals (edited with Introduction). The Viking Press, New York, 1927.

LARSEN, NELLA (MRS. IMES).
Quicksand (novel). Alfred A. Knopf, Inc., New York, 1928.
Passing (novel). Alfred A. Knopf, Inc., New York, 1929.

MCKAY, CLAUDE.
Harlem Shadows (poems). Harcourt, Brace & Co., 1922.
Home to Harlem (novel). Harper & Bros., New York and London, 1928.
Banjo (novel). Harper & Bros., New York and London, 1929.

TOOMER, JEAN: *Cane* (novel). Boni & Liveright, New York, 1923.

WALROND, ERIC.
Tropic Death (stories and sketches). Boni & Liveright, New York, 1926.
The Big Ditch. Boni & Liveright, New York, 1928.

WASHINGTON, BOOKER T.: *Up From Slavery: An Autobiography*. Doubleday, Page & Co., New York, 1901.

WHEATLEY, PHILLIS.
Poem on the Death of the Reverend George Whitefield. Boston, 1770.
Poems on Various Subjects, Religious and Moral. London and Boston, 1773.
Elegy Sacred to the Memory of Dr. Samuel Cooper. Boston, 1784.

Liberty and Peace. Boston, 1784.
Letters, edited by Charles Deane. Boston, 1864.

(Note.—The bibliography of Phillis Wheatley is now a study in itself. The volume of 1773 is now rare and valuable. Numerous reprints have been made, among them the following: Philadelphia, 1774; Philadelphia, 1786; Albany, 1793; Philadelphia, 1801; Walpole, N. H., 1802; Hartford, 1804; Halifax, 1813; "New England," 1816; Denver, 1887; Philadelphia, 1909 (A. M. E. Book Concern). Note also Memoir of Phillis Wheatley, by B. B. Thatcher, Boston, 1834; and Memoir and Poems of Phillis Wheatley (memoir by Margaretta Matilda Odell), Boston, 1834, 1835, and 1838, the three editions in rapid succession being due to the anti-slavery agitation. Not the least valuable part of Deane's edition of the Letters is the sketch of Phillis Wheatley by Nathaniel B. Shurtleff which it contains. This was first printed in *The Boston Daily Advertiser,* Dec. 21, 1863. Duyckinck's Cyclopædia of American Literature gave a good review and reprinted from *The Pennsylvania Magazine* the correspondence with Washington, the poem to Washington, and "Liberty and Peace." Also important for reference is Oscar Wegelin's Compilation of the Titles of Volumes of Verse—Early American Poetry, New York, 1903. Note also The Life and Works of Phillis Wheatley, by G. Herbert Renfro, edited by Leila Amos Pendleton, Washington, 1916. The whole matter of bibliography has been exhaustively studied in Heartman's Historical Series, in beautiful books of limited editions, as follows: (1) Phillis Wheatley: A Critical Attempt and a Bibliography of Her Writings, by Charles Fred Heartman, New York, 1915; (2) Phillis Wheatley: Poems and Letters. First Collected Edition. Edited by Charles Fred Heartman, with an Appreciation by Arthur A. Schomburg, New York, 1915; (3) Six Broadsides relating to Phillis Wheatley, New York, 1915. These books are of the first order of importance, and yet they raise one or two questions. One wonders why "To Mæcenas," "On Virtue," and "On Being Brought from Africa to America," all very early productions, were placed near the end of all the poems in "Poems and Letters"; nor is the relation between "To a Clergyman on the Death of His Lady" and "To the Rev. Mr. Pitkin on the Death of His Lady" made clear, the two poems, obviously different versions of the same thing, being placed pages apart. The great merit of the book, however, is that it adds to "Poems on Various Subjects" the four other poems not generally accessible: (1) To His Excellency, George Washington; (2) On Major-General Lee; (3) Liberty and Peace; (4) An Elegy Sacred to the Memory of Dr. Samuel Cooper.)

WHITE, WALTER F.

The Fire in the Flint (novel). Alfred A. Knopf, Inc., New York, 1924.

Flight (novel). Alfred A. Knopf, Inc., New York, 1926.

Rope and Faggot. Alfred A. Knopf, Inc., New York, 1929.

WHITMAN, ALBERY A.

Not a Man and Yet a Man (poems). Springfield, Ohio, 1877.

Twasinta's Seminoles, or The Rape of Florida (poem). Nixon-Jones Printing Co., St. Louis, Mo., 1884.

Drifted Leaves. Nixon-Jones Printing Co., St. Louis, 1890. (This brings together the two former works, adding some miscellaneous.)

An Idyl of the South, an epic poem in two parts. The Metaphysical Publishing Co., New York, 1901.

II

Other Books (Including Collections), Mainly Critical or Biographical, Not Necessarily by Negroes

BULLOCK, RALPH W.: *In Spite of Handicaps.* Association Press, New York, 1927.

CROMWELL, JOHN W.: *The Negro in American History.* The American Negro Academy, Washington, 1914.

DETT, R. NATHANIEL: *Religious Folk-Songs of the Negro.* G. Schirmer, New York and London, 1925.

HATCHER, WILLIAM E.: *John Jasper.* Fleming H. Revell Co., New York, 1908.

JOHNSON, CHARLES S. (editor) : *Ebony and Topaz: A Collectanea.* National Urban League, New York, 1927.

KERLIN, ROBERT J.: *Negro Poets and Their Poems.* The Associated Publishers, Washington, 1922.

KREHBIEL, HENRY E.: *Afro-American Folk-Songs.* G. Schirmer, New York and London, 1914.

LOCKE, ALAIN (editor).
Four Negro Poets. Simon and Schuster, New York, 1926.
The New Negro. A. C. Boni, New York, 1925.
(With Gregory, Montgomery): *Plays of Negro Life.* Harper & Bros., New York and London, 1927.

ODUM, HOWARD W., and JOHNSON, GUY B. (editors).
The Negro and His Songs. University of North Carolina Press, Chapel Hill, 1925.
Negro Workaday Songs. University of North Carolina Press, Chapel Hill, 1926.

OVINGTON, MARY WHITE: *Portraits in Color.* The Viking Press, New York, 1927.

PIKE, G. D.: *The Jubilee Singers.* Lee & Shepard. Boston, 1873.

SAYERS, W. C. BERWICK: *Samuel Coleridge-Taylor, Musician: His Life and Letters.* Cassell & Co., London and New York, 1915.

SCARBOROUGH, DOROTHY: *On the Trail of Negro Folk Songs.* Harvard University Press, Cambridge, 1925.

SCHOMBURG, ARTHUR A.: *A Bibliographical Checklist of American Negro Poetry.* New York, 1916.

TALLEY, THOMAS W.: *Negro Folk Rhymes.* The Macmillan Company, New York, 1922.

TROTTER, JAMES M.: *Music and Some Highly Musical People.* Boston, 1878.

WHITE, NEWMAN IVEY, and JACKSON, WALTER CLINTON (editors): *An Anthology of Verse by American Negroes.* Duke University Press, Durham, N. C., 1924.

Note also *Black Opals,* occasionally issued at 2220 Catherine St., Philadelphia, and *The Saturday Evening Quill,* issued annually at 32 Copley St., Cambridge, Mass.

III

Select List of Magazine Articles

(The arrangement is chronological, and articles of unusual scholarship or interest are marked *.)

* *Negro Spirituals,* by Thomas Wentworth Higginson. *Atlantic,* Vol. 19, p. 685 (June, 1867).

*The Negro on the Stage, by Laurence Hutton. *Harper's,* Vol. 79, p. 131 (June, 1889).

Old Plantation Hymns, Hymns of the Slave and the Freedman, Recent Negro Melodies; a series of three articles by William E. Barton. *New England Magazine,* Vol. 19, pp. 443, 609, 707 (December, 1898, January and February, 1899).

Mr. Charles W. Chesnutt's Stories, by W. D. Howells. *Atlantic,* Vol. 85, p. 70 (May, 1900).

Paul Laurence Dunbar, by Mary Church Terrell. *Voice of the Negro,* Vol. 3, p. 271 (April, 1906).

Dunbar's Best Book. Bookman, Vol. 23, p. 122 (April, 1906). Tribute by W. D. Howells in same issue, p. 185.

Chief Singer of the Negro Race. Current Literature, Vol. 40, p. 400 (April, 1906).

Meta Warrick, Sculptor of Horrors, by William Francis O'Donnell. *World To-day,* Vol. 13, p. 1139 (November, 1907). See also *Current Literature,* Vol. 44, p. 55 (January, 1908).

Afro-American Painter Who Has Become Famous in Paris. Current Literature, Vol. 45, p. 404 (October, 1908).

*The Story of an Artist's Life, by H. O. Tanner. *World's Work,* Vol. 18, pp. 11661, 11769 (June and July, 1909).

Indian and Negro in Music. Literary Digest, Vol. 44, p. 1346 (June 29, 1912).

The Higher Music of Negroes (mainly on Coleridge-Taylor). *Literary Digest,* Vol. 45, p. 565 (October 5, 1912).

*The Negro's Contribution to the Music of America, by Natalie Curtis. *Craftsman,* Vol. 23, p. 660 (March, 1913).

The Soul of the Black (Herbert Ward's Bronzes). *Independent,* Vol. 74, p. 994 (May 1, 1913).

A Poet Painter of Palestine (H. O. Tanner), by Clara T. MacChesney. *International Studio,* July, 1913.

The Negro in Literature and Art, by W. E. Burghardt DuBois. *Annals* of the American Academy of Political and Social Science, Vol. 49, p. 233 (September, 1913).

Beginnings of a Negro Drama. Literary Digest,
 Vol. 48, p. 1114 (May 9, 1914).

George Moses Horton: Slave Poet, by Stephen B.
 Weeks. *Southern Workman,* Vol. 43, p. 571
 (October, 1914).

The Negro in the Southern Short Story, by H. E.
 Rollins. *Sewanee Review,* Vol. 24, p. 42 (January, 1916).

**H. T. Burleigh: Composer by Divine Right, and
 the American Coleridge-Taylor. Musical Amer-
 ica,* Vol. 23, No. 26 (April 29, 1916). See also
 *An American Negro Whose Music Stirs the
 Blood of Warring Italy. Current Opinion,*
 August, 1916, p. 100.

Afro-American Folk-Song Contribution, by Maud
 Cuney Hare. *Musical Observer,* Vol. 15, No. 2,
 p. 13 (February, 1917).

The Emancipation of Negro Music, by R. Nathaniel Dett. *Southern Workman,* Vol. 47, p. 172
 (April, 1918).

Negro Patriotism and Negro Music, by Frances R.
 Grant. *Outlook,* Vol. 121, p. 343 (February 26,
 1919).

Some Contemporary Poets of the Negro Race, by
 William Stanley Braithwaite. *Crisis,* Vol. 17, p.
 275 (April, 1919).

Joel Chandler Harris and Negro Folklore, by Elsie
 Clews Parsons. *Dial,* Vol. 66, p. 491 (May 17,
 1919).

Racial Traits in the Negro Song, by N. I. White.
 Sewanee Review, (July, 1920).

Our Debt to Negro Sculpture. Literary Digest,
 (July 17, 1920).

Negro Sculpture, by C. Bell. *Living Age,* (September 25, 1920).

Present Day Negro Poets, by Robert T. Kerlin. *Southern Workman,* Vol. 49, p. 543 (December, 1920).

*Hindu Stories in American Negro Folk-lore, by W. Norman Brown. *Asia,* Vol. 21, p. 703 (August, 1921).

*Some Notes on Coleridge-Taylor, by Herbert Antcliffe. *Musical Quarterly,* Vol. 8, p. 180 (April, 1922).

The Negro in Drama, by Rollin Lynde Harte. *Crisis,* Vol. 24, p. 61 (June, 1922).

The Younger Literary Movement, by W. E. B. DuBois and Alain Locke. *Crisis,* Vol. 27, p. 161 (February, 1924).

William Edouard Scott, Painter, by Francis C. Holbrook. *Southern Workman,* Vol. 53, p. 72 (February, 1924).

*Arts and Crafts of the Negro. International Studio, Vol. 78, p. 477 (March, 1924).

Henry Ossawa Tanner, by Jessie Fauset. *Crisis,* Vol. 27, p. 255 (April, 1924).

*The Musical Genius of the American Negro, by Clarence Cameron White. *Étude,* Vol. 42, p. 305 (May, 1924).

The Negro in Literature, by William Stanley Braithwaite. *Crisis,* Vol. 28, p. 204 (September, 1924).

A World-Famous Singer Whose Parents Were Slaves (Roland Hayes), by Mary B. Mullett. *American Magazine,* June, 1925.

The Negro Literary Renaissance, by Benjamin Brawley. *Southern Workman,* Vol. 56, p. 177 (April, 1927).

George Polgren Bridgetower, by Maud Cuney Hare. *Crisis,* Vol. 34, p. 122 (June, 1927).

Negro Artists and the Negro, by Wallace Thurman. *New Republic,* Vol. 52, p. 37 (August 31, 1927).

Florence Mills. Crisis, Vol. 34, p. 229 (September, 1927).

The Negro and Musical Talent, by Guy B. Johnson. *Southern Workman,* Vol. 56, p. 439 (October, 1927).

The Vogue of the Negro Spiritual, by A. M. Chirgwin. *Edinburgh Review,* Vol. 247, p. 57 (January, 1928).

The Jewel in Ethiope's Ear, by Edwin D. Johnson. *Opportunity,* Vol. 6, p. 166 (June, 1928).

Negro Art in Europe (on Roland Hayes). *Crisis,* Vol. 36, p. 19 (January, 1929).

1928: A Retrospective Review, by Alain Locke. *Opportunity,* Vol. 7, p. 8 (January, 1929).

INDEX